CLASSIC
HARLEY-DAVIDSON
1903-1941

HERBERT WAGNER

PHOTOGRAPHY BY
MARK MITCHELL

MBI Publishing Company

DEDICATION

To the ghost rider

First published in 1999 by MBI Publishing Company,
729 Prospect Avenue, PO Box 1, Osceola, WI
54020-0001 USA.

MBI Publishing Company books are also available at
discounts in bulk quantity for industrial or sales-
promotional use. For details write to Special Sales
Manager at Motorbooks International Wholesalers &
Distributors, 729 Prospect Avenue, PO Box 1, Osceola,
WI 54020-0001 USA.

Library of Congress Cataloging-in-Publication Data

Wagner, Herbert
        Classic Harley-Davidson, 1903-1941/Herbert
Wagner and Mark Mitchell
        p. cm.-- (Enthusiast Color Series)
        Includes index.
        ISBN 0-7603-0557-9 (pbk. : alk. paper)
        1. Harley-Davidson Motorcycle--History.
        I. Mitchell, Mark
TL448.H3W3396   1999
629.227'5--dc21   98-48453

On the front cover: **This VL with a side-valve 74-cubic-inch engine is owned by the Bluegrass Museum in Kentucky.**

On the frontispiece: **The overhead-valve Peashooter was Harley's first engine with a hemispherical combustion chamber.**

On the title page: **Owned by Mike Terry, this is an original-condition 1913 single with acetylene lighting and an acetylene tank mounted on the handlebars.**

On the back cover: **Pictured here is the 1936 EL, complete with the deluxe chrome package.**

Edited by Greg Field
Designed by Tom Heffron

Printed in Hong Kong

CONTENTS

FOREWORD

Herbert Wagner is one of the few who can rightfully be called a historian. Scholars can obtain the facts—which Mr. Wagner does with precision—but only historians can reveal the narratives that facts will often conceal from the less inspired.

Classic Harley-Davidson, 1903–1941 is a remarkable book for its Logos and Mythos. During his investigations for this text, Herbert Wagner worked closely with the Harley-Davidson Archives to study primary and secondary materials that would not have been available elsewhere, and to converse with Archives personnel with whom many spirited discussions took place regarding the materials. Some of Wagner's findings were so serendipitous that upon discovery he said to me, "Marty, the ghost just walked through the room!"

Information on historical overhead-valve technology was, I believe, the moment when Herbert's ghost was released, but it could have been set free to haunt during any number of his discoveries. The Archives' antique motorcycle, photograph, literature, and ephemera collections contain the very essence of the phenomenon we all know as Harley-Davidson.

I am pleased that it could be utilized for this book, and now it is time for you, the reader, to let the ghost walk through your room as you read Herbert Wagner's brilliant historical incantation.

Dr. Martin Jack Rosenblum
Historian
Harley-Davidson Motor Company

ACKNOWLEDGMENTS

The author's historical research on the Harley-Davidson Motor Co. has been conducted continuously since 1988. Material for this book came from a variety of published and unpublished sources. The latter includes letters, taped interviews, original factory data, notes, photographs, and other information from the author's files.

The author wishes to thank the following persons for assistance with the present book: Mrs. Bill Borer, Bob Chantland, Alfred Embretsen, Greg Field, Aaron Fitch (of the Motorcycle Heritage Museum), Herb Glass, Chris Haynes, Bob Jameson, Mark Jonas, Tom Jorsch, Akemi Somon Kobayashi, Walter Kobs, Joe Koller, Rachel Amara Landman, Arnold Meyer Jr., Fritz Meyer, Mark

Mitchell and Rebecca Dobyns, Rick Morsher, Elizabeth Durr Moyle, Adolph Roemer, Phil Runser (of Advanced Cycle Machining), the late George Sceets, Connie Schlemmer, Dr. Mark Sneed, Joseph Somogyi family, Daniel Statnekov, Grace Kobs Valsano, Howard Vandegrift, the late Tom Vandegrift, Mrs. Walter Waech, Mark Wall, Tom Wagner, the late John Warner, and Dick Werner.

Special thanks to the John E. Harley family for preserving and sharing the 1901 engine drawing, R. L. Jones for information on hillclimbers and early racers, Mike Lange for his intimate knowledge of early Harley engines, Bruce Linsday for his expertise on the first Harleys and his boundless enthusiasm for Knuckleheads, Floyd Smith for help on the classic hillclimbing scene, and to Chuck Wesholski for introducing me to the super-important Two-Cam/OHV and straightening me out about the Knuth's Special.

And last, but certainly not least, thanks to Tom Bolfert, Bill Jackson, Dr. Martin Jack Rosenblum, and Ray Schlee for their great assistance at the Harley-Davidson Archives on Juneau Avenue in Milwaukee.

—Herbert Wagner

INTRODUCTION

Between 1903 and 1941 the modern Harley-Davidson motorcycle came into existence. From a spindly, single-cylinder razorstrap job, the Harley grew into the 74 OHV Big Twin—the Knucklehead—a fast, reliable roadburner still worthy of the pavement today.

This development began shortly after the close of the American frontier. Having conquered the lower 48 states, that restless American spirit set out to invent the best means of exploring them. For four young men in Milwaukee, Wisconsin, this meant the motorcycle. By 1941 their motorized bicycle had become an iron horse.

Yet mysteries remain about Harley-Davidson's early history. What originally inspired Bill Harley and Arthur Davidson to build a motorcycle? What did their 1901 motor-bicycle engine look like? Where did the big motor and loop frame of 1903 come from? When was the first twin built? Why did Harley-Davidson grow so quickly in the early years? What part did World War I play? When did the image of the anti-social biker first appear? Why was the 21-cubic-inch Single significant? What unknown experimental model inspired the Knucklehead? When were the first Knuckleheads shipped from the factory? Was there a single-cylinder Knucklehead?

This book tries to answer these and other questions in the colorful setting of Mark Mitchell's photographs. The history of Harley-Davidson might be termed a mechanical romance. In these pages, I've attempted to explore a part of that romance for Harley-Davidson enthusiasts everywhere.

CHAPTER 1

PENNINGTON'S MOTORCYCLE, TWO FRENCHMEN, AND THE 1901 BICYCLE MOTOR

In another life. Bill Harley might have been an artist and Arthur Davidson a cattle rancher. But things turned out differently. For in the summer of 1895. Edward Joel "Airship" Pennington touched down in Milwaukee with his fabulous new invention: the "Motor Cycle."

This was the day of the bicycle craze, and millions of American men and women were on wheels. But the bicycle was limited to the power in one's legs. Hills were a bitch. Some dreamers were asking for the seemingly impossible: a motorized bicycle.

> **"The greatest possibilities are with the bicycle, driven by electric power or compressed air, by which means . . . fifty miles an hour will soon be reached."**
>
> —Alfred Wallace, 1896
> *The Wonderful Century*

Over the years, there had been a few steam-powered velocipedes. In 1885 Germany. Daimler had built a gasoline-powered hobby-horse. but with four wheels this device was not a true motorcycle. H-D's historian. Marty Rosenblum, has aptly dubbed it "the first Volkswagen."

Nor did these early freaks capture the imagination of the dreamers, those who grasped the essence of a true motorcycle: light, strong, nimble, powerful, fast, and handsome. As if answering their prayers, Pennington arrived, messiah-like, with his prophetic Motor Cycle.

This Indiana-born inventor-promoter had invented a compact type of gasoline engine he then fitted to the rear frame section of a bicycle. The connecting rods operated, locomotive-style, directly upon the rear wheel hub. Pennington claimed that his 12-pound engine produced 2 horsepower.

The French de Dion-Bouton engine set the pattern for the first successful motorcycles. This 1 3/4-horsepower 1899 example with close-set rear wheels is owned by Reed Martin and was ordered by the Vanderbilts for use as a bicycle pacer.

9

FIG. 15.   [From the *Engineer.*

Pennington's "Motor Cycle" was seen in several American cities before it came to Milwaukee in 1895. Bill Harley and Arthur Davidson—then both 14 years old—lived just a few blocks from where the Motor Cycle was publicly demonstrated. AUTHOR COLLECTION

Loud, crude, and imperfect, the Motor Cycle drew crowds wherever it went. By 1890s standards, it moved with "lightning-like rapidity," according to one Milwaukee newspaper. It held infinite possibilities at a time when the bicycle itself bordered upon the magical.

In Milwaukee, Pennington made two dashes up and down Wisconsin Avenue, leaving the street awash in a haze of poorly combusted hydrocarbons, raw gasoline, the bark of exhaust, and Pennington's own booming bombast. Police could scarcely hold back the crowd. Later, Pennington claimed that he did 58 miles per hour in Milwaukee—his best speed to date.

At this point an important historical question arises: Who was in the crowd that day? For just a few blocks from this fantastic 1890s scene there lived two families named Harley and Davidson.

William Sylvester Harley and Arthur Davidson were boyhood chums. In 1895 they were 14 years old. At this impressionable age both were keenly interested in mechanical things and optimistic for the birth of a new century.

It's hardly conceivable that two young Milwaukee lads, living near the scene of Pennington's ride, failed to witness this historic event. Subsequent Harley-Davidson histories tell of a dream these two boys had of building a motorized bicycle long before they actually did so. Might this dream have sprouted from their encounter with that knuckle-head genius E. J. Pennington?

But the Motor Cycle of 1895 was a flash on the horizon, then gone. After that one-day visit, Milwaukee settled back into its late-19th-century beery slumber.

But events had been set in motion. The next year the Harley family moved to the north side where young William found employment at the Meiselbach bicycle factory. The Davidsons moved to the city's western outskirts, and Art went to Cambridge, Wisconsin, where he lived on his grandmother's farm. There he met another gaso-line-sniffing pioneer, Ole Oleson Evinrude.

Across the ocean, other developments were taking place that would transform the motorcycle from a charlatan's contraption into a practical device. This achievement was due to two Frenchmen: the brilliant Comte Albert de Dion and his wizard-like mechanic, Georges Bouton.

Confident that the future of *l'idée automobile* rested in gasoline, de Dion and former-toy-maker Bouton began experimenting with the Daimler-Maybach version of Otto's four-stroke engine. Using hot-tube ignition, Daimler's vertical, all-enclosed 212 cc engine produced 1/2 horsepower at 600 rpm, but weighed 189 pounds.

De Dion and Bouton did better. By miniaturizing Daimler's motor, they created an air-cooled engine that weighed just 40 pounds. They also developed a new form of battery/spark ignition utilizing a cam-activated circuit breaker run off the engine. Now the spark could keep pace with the piston as rpm increased. This allowed the de Dion-Bouton engine to spin at unheard-of rates. When tested in 1895, this 137 cc engine took off like a rocket to 3,000 rpm and ran *reliably* at 1,500, producing about 1/2 horsepower.

A revolution in gasoline engineering had taken place. With the de Dion-Bouton engine the modern motorcycle was possible. Every bike engine today is derived from this motor. Ironically, Pennington later claimed that *his* engine had inspired de Dion-Bouton's work, but this was probably wishful thinking.

After 1896, de Dion tricycles and quadracycles filled Paris boulevards. French motor-bicycles appeared in 1897. This new technology reached the United States in 1898, with clones of the de Dion trike. But trikes couldn't easily negotiate rutted American roads. Two-wheelers could. The first *successful* American motorcycles—the Thomas, Marsh, and Orient—appeared in late 1900. Predictably, these bikes showed a strong French influence, as would the first Indian.

By this time Bill Harley was an apprentice draftsman at the Barth Manufacturing Co. Writing to his pal Art Davidson out on the farm, he told of the big demand for skilled workers in Milwaukee's booming industries. Taking Harley's advice, Art came home and became an apprentice pattern maker.

One evening they went to the Bijou Theater and witnessed Anna Held, the Parisian-born come-dienne, whiz across the stage on a nickel-plated French motor-bicycle.

The eyes of our young titans bugged out at the sight of this "shapely damsel in white tights" maneuvering around the stage. As they recalled 41 years later in the *Milwaukee Journal*, "It was just one of those many little things that push people further toward a goal they are groping for."

The motorcycle of 1900 had not yet reached Milwaukee streets, but with this new inspiration, Bill Harley and Arthur Davidson decided to build their own.

It was an ambitious project to start from scratch. Luckily, do-it-yourself engine kits were becoming available. From a magazine ad you could purchase the rough castings and on a lathe make motor shafts and other parts. You could then clamp the finished engine onto a bicycle and drive it with belt and pulley. Harley and Davidson apparently took this first step in their career of building motorcycles.

A 1914 newspaper article tells that a German-born "draughtsman," working in the same machine shop as our heroes, gave them valuable technical advice on gasoline engines. Another break came when Henry Melk, a pal in Bill Harley's neighborhood, let them use his lathe.

Facts were sketchy about this first Harley-Davidson motor until 1997, when an engineering drawing of it surfaced. This oldest known H-D relic

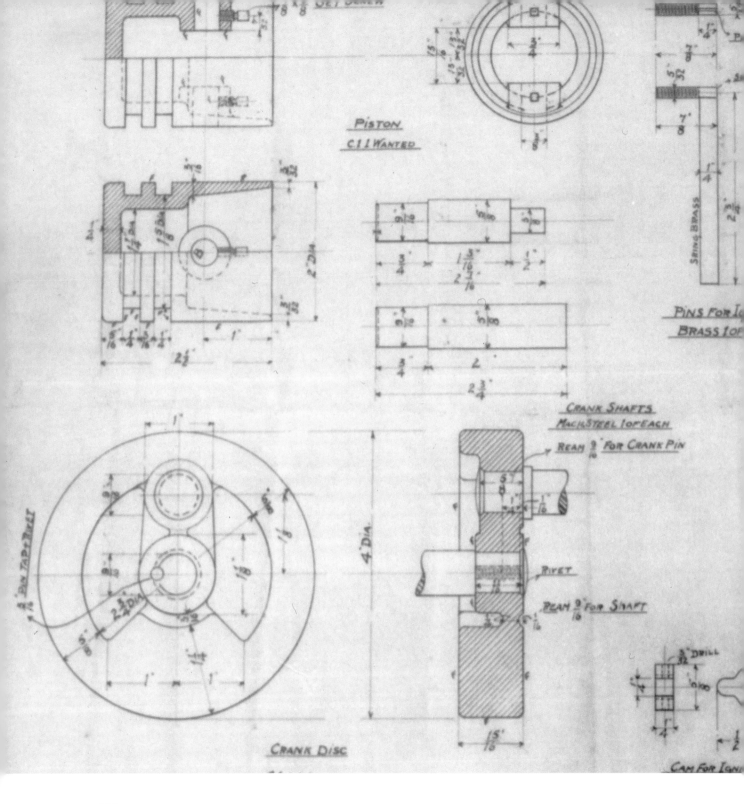

PISTON

C.I. WANTED

PINS FOR IG...

BRASS 1 OF...

CRANK SHAFTS

MACH. STEEL 1 OF EACH

REAM $\frac{9}{16}$" FOR CRANK PIN

RIVET

REAM $\frac{9}{16}$" FOR SHAFT

CRANK DISC

CAM FOR IGNI...

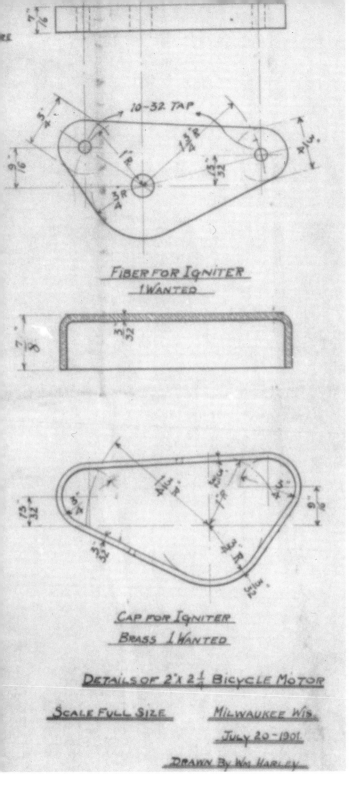

FIBER FOR IGNITER
1 WANTED

CAP FOR IGNITER
BRASS 1 WANTED

DETAILS OF 2" X 2¼ BICYCLE MOTOR

SCALE FULL SIZE   MILWAUKEE WIS.

JULY 20 -1901

DRAWN BY WM HARLEY

is dated July 20, 1901, and is signed by William S. Harley. The drawing is labeled "Sheet 2," and shows several parts of the bicycle motor. For unknown reasons its 2x2 1/4-inch bore and stroke (7.068 cubic inches or 115.8 cc) with 4-inch flywheels differs from those described in the 1914 *Milwaukee Journal* article, which states, "the first motor had a bore of 2 1/8 inches and a stroke of 2 7/8 inches, the fly wheel being 5 inches in diameter."

The 1901 drawing does show, however, that production Harley-Davidson engines of 1903–1905 were *not* enlarged versions of this first design. A comparison between the dimensions on the cast parts versus the machined parts suggests that this 1901 engine was built around a purchased kit. Early-Harley expert Bruce Linsday observed, "Looks like [Harley] measured the castings he had in his hand, and was pretty vague on the machined parts that still had to be made."

This kit approach to engine building was a logical choice for two young guys with little money, no experience, and access only to Henry Melk's lathe. Ambition, however, they had in abundance, and late in 1901 they installed the motor in an ordinary bicycle chassis and tested their invention. To their dismay they found it too weakly powered for climbing Milwaukee's steeper hills.

We can only imagine their disappointment. By then—late 1901—motorcycles were reality on Milwaukee streets, where A. J. Monday was handling the Thomas brand. In nearby Racine, the Wisconsin Wheel Works was turning out the Mitchell motorcycle. On Milwaukee's south side, Joe Merkel was building Merkel motorcycles.

At that juncture Bill Harley and Art Davidson might have thrown in the towel. Why should they build a motorcycle of their own when they could just go out and buy one?

This engineering drawing signed by William S. Harley is dated July 20, 1901. It shows parts for a 7.07-cubic-inch (116 cc) bicycle motor. When put into a frame, this engine was found lacking in power for Milwaukee hills, but inspired bigger motors to come. PHOTO COURTESY JOHN E. HARLEY FAMILY

Bill Harley and Arthur Davidson weren't easily discouraged. Davidson, a brassy little guy, was no quitter. Building a motorcycle was more art than science anyway, and there was plenty of artist in Bill Harley.

The motor-bicycle project had given them valuable experience. Examining the motorcycles being built, they were determined to do better next time. Plus they had friends. Among them was a man who later became famous for outboard motors, Ole Evinrude.

Ole was three years older than Bill Harley and Arthur Davidson and considerably more worldly. He had worked in machine shops in Madison, Pittsburgh, and Chicago. Nights, he studied books on gasoline engineering, and soon he began experimenting.

By 1902, Ole was in business with Frank Clemick on Florida Street in Milwaukee. The Clemick-Evinrude Co. billed themselves as "pattern makers and engine builders." Their engine

> "Everyone . . . was fooling around with motors and gasoline that evaporated faster than it drove those motors. Nothing ran smoothly but the whole thing was exciting, like coming into a new world of green valleys and blue mountains."
>
> —Gustave Pabst, Jr.

was Ole's adaptation of the de Dion-Bouton type—in water-cooled form—for automotive use.

At that time Ole was developing an improved engine. In 1903, he formed a new partnership to market it with Ferdy Achtenhagen at 255 Lake Street. This was the Motor Car Power Equipment Co.

Here's where things got interesting. Not only was Ole a friend of Art Davidson from their Cambridge days, but Art was also a "partner" in Ole's pattern shop around this time. Just two blocks away, Bill Harley was working at Pawling & Harnischfeger.

Since 1914, Harley-Davidson has given credit to Evinrude for helping our heroes get a start, usually with their carburetor. But Ole's help appears to have gone deeper. Several unique features of Evinrude's improved motor are found in early Harley-Davidson engines. These include the hand starter, two-piece exhaust valve, side exhaust port, roller tappet, and oil routing system to the crankpin. The last two features are still used on Harley-Davidson engines today.

Coincidence? Not likely, considering the close connections between these guys. It's easy to surmise what happened. With the puny 1901 motor a failure, big-hearted Ole probably encouraged Bill Harley to draft plans for an air-cooled cycle engine from his larger water-cooled design. A case of one great man helping another get his start.

"Negative 599." This circa-1912 photo was labeled "1903 Harley-Davidson" and shows a bike with pre-1905 features. The spring fork was added later. The bike was probably sold in 1904 to Henry Meyer and by 1912 had accumulated 100,000 miles. Its current whereabouts are unknown. PHOTO COURTESY MILWAUKEE COUNTY HISTORICAL SOCIETY

The timing is right. Both men were working on new engines in 1902; both finished them in 1903. Yet, while showing strong Evinrude influence, the H-D was not a direct copy. The Evinrude motor was water-cooled and larger, the crankcases were heavier and reinforced, and lubrication was by oil cup. It should also be remembered that all these early engines were copies of the de Dion-Bouton, which in turn was based on Daimler's design.

The improved Harley-Davidson motor of 1902–1903 more than doubled the displacement of the previous bicycle motor. Bore and stroke were 3x3 1/2 inches, yielding 24.74 cubic inches (405 cc). The flywheels were 9 3/4 inches, *not* 11 1/2 inches as incorrectly reported in 1914 and repeated ever since. Output was about 3 horsepower.

With an engine worthy of the name "Harley-Davidson," our young mechanics were eager to push ahead—only to discover a new hurdle.

The 1901 motor had been small enough to install on an ordinary bicycle frame, standard practice at that time. But at 49 pounds, the 1902–1903 motor was too large for similar treatment. Luckily, rapid advances in the local motorcycle industry provided the answer. Thereby hangs an untold tale, and a big part of Harley-Davidson's early success.

The big name in the early motorcycle industry was the Indian Motocycle Co. of Springfield, Massachusetts. With its low-slung engine inline with the seat post in a bicycle-style diamond frame, the Indian was maneuverable, light, and speedy. The original 1901 design was so successful that Indian stuck to it until 1909, long after it was obsolete.

In the Milwaukee area, however, the two earliest builders took a less successful initial approach. Both the (Milwaukee) Merkel and (Racine) Mitchell models of 1901–1902 utilized bicycle-style frames with high-mounted engines. While racy looking, these proved a devil for sideslip.

Consequently, both these companies came out with entirely new designs for 1903. These new Merkel and Mitchell machines were highly advanced, second-generation mounts. Abandoning the diamond-shaped bicycle chassis, both firms introduced frames in which the engine was the integral heart of the vehicle instead of showing a tacked-on bicycle approach. This design philosophy is universally followed today.

The 1903 Merkel used the classic "loop frame" style where the front down tube wrapped around the engine crankcase and then looped up as the seat post. The 1903 Mitchell utilized a slightly different "cradle frame" in which the front down tube flowed back as the rear frame-stay instead of that section being added separately. Both makes mounted their engines low and with a forward cant to allow better cylinder cooling.

The innovative 1903 Merkel and Mitchell designs took into account the physics of mating the gasoline engine to the two-wheeler. Forward thinkers realized that motorcycles were not motorized bicycles, but unique vehicles with their own demands and solutions.

Here, too, timing is significant. In late 1902, when these advanced designs were being introduced by Milwaukee-area factories, Bill Harley and

The Merkel motorcycle was built in Milwaukee between 1901 and 1908. The first Harley may have been inspired by the re-designed 1903 model, as the frames are nearly identical and overall styling very similar. No examples of this model Merkel is known to survive. AUTHOR COLLECTION

Arthur Davidson were searching for a better chassis for their improved motor. They apparently found it in the Merkel loop frame, as the early Harley-Davidson frame is a dead ringer.

This is all vital stuff. It allowed the prototype Harley-Davidson of 1903 to appear as a second-generation mount—a true motorcycle utilizing the best of current theory and practice. With a superior engine and frame, Harley-Davidson was propelled rapidly forward while others were struggling with underpowered, obsolete, or freakish designs.

Patterns for the improved model were made by Arthur Davidson, based on Bill Harley's drawings. Machine work was done on Henry Melk's lathe. It's also likely that Art's older brother, William A. Davidson, began lending a hand as well. Real old-timers still chuckle when they recall Bill Davidson—in 1903 the toolroom foreman at the West Milwaukee car shops of the Chicago, Milwaukee & St. Paul Railway—telling how parts for the first Harley were fabricated at the railroad. He jokingly referred to it as "government work."

This makes perfect sense. Material had to be obtained. Parts such as the flywheels called for big equipment. Others had to be cast. The flywheel cutouts in early H-D motors resemble a locomotive's drive wheel. Coincidence? Maybe, but consider how many skilled men later followed Bill Davidson from the railroad, and it's no mystery that much of the first Harley came out of the railshops. Today, these buildings stand as ruins below the 35th Street viaduct in Milwaukee.

The individual parts were assembled into a complete motorcycle in the backyard "woodshed" of the Davidson family home at 315 37th Street (now 38th Street). The shed was originally built by the Davidson boys' father, William C. Davidson, for his own use, but was soon taken over by his sons and Bill Harley.

Early histories tell that in April 1903, Walter Davidson came back to Milwaukee for brother Bill's marriage to Mary Bauer. Walter was enticed to join their budding motorcycle-building enterprise by the promise of a ride. One 1916 source largely credits Walter with building the 1903 prototype.

Their new machine drew considerable attention. From nearby Vliet Street, the Becker boys started

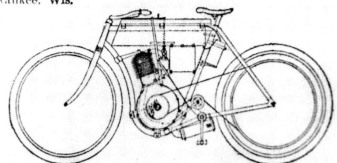

Harley-Davidson Motor Cycle

Made by Harley-Davidson Motor Co., 315 37th St., Milwaukee, Wis.

HARLEY-DAVIDSON MOTOR CYCLE. PRICE $175.

21½-inch frame; 2-inch tires, but option is given on 2¼-inch; 51½-inch wheel base; single cylinder, 3⅛x3½; 3¼ H. P. motor; centrifugal eight feed lubrication;

This line drawing, published in April 1905, may portray the first Harley-Davidson or the 1904 factory racer. It is the earliest known visual representation of a Harley-Davidson motorcycle and another of Bill Harley's artistic renderings. AUTHOR COLLECTION

hanging around. Interested guys from the railshops, such as Max Kobs, stopped by, as did schoolyard chums like Henry Meyer. Everybody lent a hand when needed and had plenty of advice to offer.

With this encouragement, the first Harley-Davidson was successfully tested in late 1903. Ten years later Bill Harley recalled the launching: "You should have seen the spark plug—as big as a door knob. And they cost us $3 each. . . . I have had a good many laughs since whenever I think of those door knob spark plugs."

It's difficult for us today to imagine the thrill this new world of motorcycles possessed. With just a little gasoline you were zooming along effortlessly toward the setting sun. The burden of pedaling had been conquered.

With the completion of their motorcycle, Bill Harley and the Davidson brothers had accomplished their task. They may have planned to fabricate another example or two so they all could ride, but surely this would be the end of their motorcycle building. Now their spare time could be spent on great outdoor adventures.

17

Thus far, creating the Harley-Davidson motorcycle had been a hobby. Then Henry Meyer got tired of walking to his job at the woolen mill and offered to buy that first 1903 machine.

This opened our heroes' eyes. The motorcycle, relatively simple to build and lower cost, was seen as a poor man's automobile. Others wanted motorcycles for speed thrills. Whatever the reason, demand outstripped supply, and overnight a hobby became an enterprise.

This resulted in the Harley-Davidson Motor Co. being formed as a partnership. Not that it meant much. All involved kept their day jobs except for Bill Harley who, realizing that he would need an engineering background to succeed in this new gasoline-powered world order, packed his spare shirt and enrolled at the University of Wisconsin in late 1903.

In 1904, one or two more Harley-Davidsons were assembled. Some claim eight, but that seems overly optimistic. They really got going in 1905. In January, and for several months thereafter, a 1-inch

"We are now offering . . . a motor that is very powerful . . . that will stand the hardest of usage with a minimum of repair."
—1905 H-D sales brochure

advertisement for "Harley-Davidson Motor Cycle Motors" was run in the *Cycle and Automobile Trade Journal*. A sales brochure was also prepared.

It's unknown how many bare motors were sold in 1905. One order from Nebraska called for fifty. Some motors were used to power boats on Pewaukee Lake.

A 1905 Harley-Davidson engine sold for $60 (carburetor $10 extra). It weighed 49 pounds—24 pounds in the motor's hefty flywheels. Good workmanship and high-quality materials were evident. Motors could be ordered with a drive pulley of 4 1/2-, 5 1/4-, or 6-inch diameter—all for use with a 1 1/4-inch flat belt. Unusual for a motorcycle engine was its provision for a hand-crank starter.

The cylinder, head, and valve chamber were integrally cast of "fine gray" iron with 1-inch cooling fins. The crankcase was made of nickel aluminum and fitted with phosphor-bronze plain bearings.

The connecting rod was constructed with a split bearing at the crank pin for taking up wear. The piston had three rings cut with a lap joint and re-turned to fit the cylinder bore.

Lubrication was by "centrifugal feed" where oil was fed by gravity from the tank to the crankpin bearing via drilled flywheel and motor shaft. From there, oil was thrown by centrifugal

For decades this racy little number was hidden behind fenders and other incorrect parts. New research led to the stunning transformation shown here. Opinions on year of manufacture vary from 1903 to 1905. *HARLEY-DAVIDSON ARCHIVES*

force to the various working parts of the motor. The system was described as "simple and efficient" with little danger of flooding the cylinder with oil.

The spark plug was placed in the side of the combustion chamber where it was less prone to fouling and overheating. The ignition circuit breaker ("interrupter") consisted of two platinum points operated by a hardened cam.

Valve openings were reported in 1905 as being 1 3/16 inches in diameter. The inlet valve was steel, while the exhaust valve had a steel stem and a cast-iron head to resist scaling. Both valves in the 1905 motor were reported as having flat seats.

From its Daimler and de Dion-Bouton ancestry, the H-D engine inherited the inlet-valve-over-exhaust-valve, head-cylinder design. Obsolete today, the IOE or F-head valve layout was used universally in the pioneer days.

In this engine type, the valves were located in an adjacent chamber or pocket at the top of the

As now restored, this early Harley resembles the engineering line drawing done by Bill Harley before April 1905. Small number "1"s on several parts led H-D to name the bike "Serial Number One." See related sidebar on page 25.

HARLEY-DAVIDSON ARCHIVES

The side exhaust and internal features of the 1905 single suggest help from Ole Evinrude. Black was standard fare in 1905 with Renault gray an option in 1906. *BIKE COURTESY **H-D** ARCHIVES.*

cylinder. The exhaust valve was aligned parallel with the bore and faced upward into the combustion chamber, while the inlet valve was positioned directly over the exhaust valve with its head facing downward into the combustion chamber. This was a practical design with several advantages—one being that fresh incoming fuel cooled the exhaust valve head, thereby reducing its temperature and failure rate.

A peculiar feature of these early F-head engines was their "automatic"-type inlet valve.

Held closed by a weak spring, the inlet valve was opened during the intake stroke of the piston when vacuum in the chamber overpowered the tension of the weak spring, opening the valve and allowing the fresh fuel charge to be sucked in. The exhaust valve was mechanically operated by a cam and closed by spring pressure, as in modern practice.

Changes were already evident between the 1903–1904 Harley-Davidson engine and the model of 1905. The previous autumn, Arthur Davidson made new patterns, and the engine was slightly

Big crankcases contain 9 3/4-inch flywheels, not 11-inch as widely reported. Heavy flywheels and relatively large displacement gave the first Harleys "lugging" advantage over the competition on poor roads.

redesigned. Engine mounting lugs were spaced farther apart for greater strength and the bore was increased from 3 to 3 1/8 inches for more power. This provided the 1905 motor with 26.84 cubic inches (440 cc), developing 3 1/4 horsepower.

In 1905, the Motor Company laid down its design philosophy by stating in its sales brochure: "Experience has shown that it is preferable to use a comparatively large motor running at a moderate speed in preference to a smaller motor running at high speed."

These first singles laid the foundation for subsequent Harley-Davidson engines. The bottom end in these early motors bears a haunting resemblance to Harley-Davidson engines today.

In June 1905, Perry E. Mack (possibly H-D's first employee) set a speed record on a local track riding a 1905 model. Afterwards (a local paper stated), Arthur Davidson walked around "swelled up like a toy balloon." This event spurred them to drop the bare motor trade for a serious attempt at building complete motorcycles.

Another impetus came when Carl Herman Lang of Chicago was in Milwaukee on business and saw their advanced motorcycle. Already a motorcycle buff, Lang offered to be their Chicago agent. Production in 1905 was probably five bikes and Lang took three, thereby becoming the world's first Harley-Davidson dealer.

These events explain why Harley's early numbering system used 1905 as base-year one. This lasted until 1916, when the current year method was adopted. Thus, a 1915 bike was designated "Model 11," 1914 bikes "Model 10," and so on back to 1905 and "Model 1." Harley-Davidson considered 1903–1904 bikes prototypes, not production machines.

Bare motor ads disappeared in mid-1905. Later that year, H-D issued its first motorcycle sales brochure with illustrations of a 1905 model. The brochure was undated and intended to serve for an indefinite period.

Bikes were offered in black in 1905, with Renault gray an option in 1906. With its motor "hung low" in the frame, the Harley-Davidson was advertised as being "especially strong to stand the rough American roads." The three-coil saddle promised to make "an ideal, easy riding machine for touring." Cost of the 1905 model was $200.

Compared to local and national competitors, the Harley-Davidson stood up well:

Belonging to the Harley Archives, and on display at the Milwaukee Public Museum, this 1907 model shows the gradual updating that marked subsequent H-D engineering history. The spring fork appears to be from a 1908 model.

Selected 1905 Models
(Cycle and Automobile Trade Journal)

Mitchell (Racine, Wis.)
Motor: 38.48 cubic inches (630 cc)
Output: 4 horsepower
Frame: cradle
Wheelbase: 55 inches
Weight: 160 pounds
Drive: chain washer belt
Top speed: 60 miles per hour

Harley-Davidson (Milwaukee, Wis.)
Motor: 26.84 cubic inches (440 cc)
Output: 3 1/4 horsepower
Frame: loop
Wheelbase: 51 inches
Weight: 138 pounds
Drive: flat belt
Top speed: 50 miles per hour

Indian (Springfield, Mass.)
Motor: 15.85 cubic inches (260 cc)
Output: 1 3/4 horsepower
Frame: diamond
Wheelbase: (not available)
Weight: 110 pounds
Drive: chain
Top speed: 40 miles per hour

Merkel (Milwaukee, Wis.)
Motor: 15.56 cubic inches (255 cc)
Output: 2 1/4 horsepower
Frame: loop
Wheelbase: 50 inches
Weight: 108 pounds
Drive: flat belt
Top speed: 35 miles per hour

This close-up view of a 1907 engine reveals subtle differences from the 1905 version. Six-bolt crankcases were found on 1906 and earlier motors, while 1907 and later had eight-bolt crankcases. Cast-in name and motor-mount position were also changed.

WORLD'S OLDEST HARLEY

The oldest motorcycle in the Harley-Davidson Archives' bike collection is well known to enthusiasts both from photographs and its display in the lobby at the Juneau Avenue headquarters.

Few questioned the lobby bike's authenticity until it was examined by Harley's professional restorer Ray Schlee in preparation for H-D's 95th Anniversary. Schlee was aided in his research on the bike by H-D's historian Marty Rosenblum and outside experts Bruce Linsday and Mike Lange. The author also contributed his two cents worth.

Based on their findings, Schlee's restoration resulted in the stunning machine pictured on pages 18 and 19. Previously, the bike had an endearing but clunky look. It was discovered, however, upon disassembly, that the bike originally had no fenders and that other key parts were incorrect, including both seat and handlebars. In addition, the engine had a higher compression than other existing pre-1906 engines, suggesting—of all things—a racing motor!

These findings were difficult to reconcile with the lobby bike's traditional configuration, save for two significant findings: First, an engineering line drawing done by William S. Harley before April 1905 shows a Harley-Davidson motorcycle *without* fenders, with low handlebars, and a low racing seat.

Second, the recently documented fact that Harley-Davidson had raced a bike in the autumn of 1904. Tying these two things together is the opinion of experts like Bruce Linsday who believes that Bill Harley's line drawing portrayed an early racer.

H-D's historian Marty Rosenblum (standing) and old-bike expert Ray Schlee played key roles in transforming the world's oldest Harley to its current, more authentic form. They are shown here with the Archives' 1905 model.

While the pros don't usually base full restorations on a solitary drawing, and Motor Company policy is to preserve, not restore, Archives bikes, this was a special case. Harley-Davidson wanted total authenticity in a bike known to be incorrect, probably dating back to circumstances in 1915 when the collection nucleus was assembled.

The line drawing—done by Bill Harley himself—was obviously authentic. Plus it was impossible to ignore the many incongruities on the lobby bike that seemed to match the line drawing bike. What tipped the scales, perhaps, was the fact that Harley raced in late 1904, and the lobby bike's motor seemed to be a racing engine. Was it possible that the stodgy old lobby bike was actually *Harley's first racer?*

As a result of these factors (and with considerable trepidation because you don't mess lightly with Harley-Davidson tradition), Schlee restored the lobby bike with a new and different look—one more in line with Bill Harley's early drawing. Depending on the bike's date of manufacture (opinions vary between 1903 and 1905), it may be the very machine ridden by Edward Hildebrand in the 1904 race. As noted previously, the higher compression motor does suggest a competition machine.

Several small number "1"s appearing on certain parts have led to serious discussion about whether this bike was the first in some series. While questions are likely to remain about this earliest known Harley, it now sports its (probable) original racy look. Whoever dreamed the first Harleys were such cool little hot rods?

The 1910 Model 6 was the last year of the "Beehive"-style motor, enlarged in 1909 to 30.17 cubic inches (495 cc). The exhaust port had migrated toward the front of the cylinder and a Schebler carburetor replaced H-D's own make. Owner Walt Richie.

New for 1910 was an improved belt tensioner with working parts behind the pulley. A single movement of the lever engaged the engine to the drive belt but was still not a practical clutch. Pedal-assist was used for the first few feet to get things rolling.

Although history books state otherwise, the Harley-Davidson engine was *not* the largest single-cylinder motor used in early American motorcycles. That distinction belongs to the "monstrous mile-a-minute Mitchell," displacing 36 percent *more* swept piston volume than the Harley. The only thing bigger in 1905 was the 42.41-cubic-inch (695 cc) Curtiss V-twin.

The Harley's appeal is evident, however, when compared to the obsolete yet popular Indian design and the advanced but sedate Merkel. The Mitchell—a real he-man's machine—was dropped in 1906 when the company shifted emphasis to auto building. After a short, disastrous foray into the auto industry, Joe Merkel left Milwaukee in 1908. But before the local industry fell apart, an interesting event took place.

Back in the autumn of 1904, a Harley-Davidson motorcycle had gone up against the Mitchell, Merkel, and other makes in the first race ever run by a Harley-Davidson motorcycle. Ridden by Edward Hildebrand, the Harley beat several makes, including the Milwaukee Merkel. But in both races the Harley was bested, first by Frank X. Zirbes of Racine on a

Mitchell, and in the other by Paul Stamser of Muskegon, Michigan, on an Indian.

Clearly, this race puts to rest the long-held myth that Harley-Davidson was not involved in racing in the early years. For already in 1904—the earliest days of its existence—we find Harley-Davidson in the thick of it.

CHAPTER 4
FACTORY EXPANSION AND
THE HARLEY-DAVIDSON TWIN

Growth came quickly to the Harley-Davidson Motor Company. In 1906, the woodshed factory turned out about 50 motorcycles. But even tripled in size, and with a drill press and lathe, the woodshed wasn't enough. With an eye toward the future, the founders purchased a lot on Chestnut Street (now Juneau Avenue) and constructed a 20x60-foot wooden building.

With a loan from a Scottish bachelor uncle, bank loans, and the sale of stock after their 1907 incorporation, H-D began to seriously expand. That fall, Bill Harley graduated from college with a degree in mechanical engineering.

Over the winter of 1907–1908, the Juneau Avenue factory received a second story and a general sprucing up. In 1908, a two-story brick addition was added to the building's west side. In 1909, the wooden two-story section was faced

> **"The buildings of the Harley-Davidson Motor Co. are built to last forever."**
> —Meyer Construction Co.'s concrete engineer, 1912

with brick and a 90x120-foot machine shop was added to the factory's east side.

This first substantial Harley-Davidson plant was built of the same buff-colored brick that gave Milwaukee its nickname of "Cream City." It was known to old-timers as the "yellow brick factory."

Company officers believed this facility would be sufficient for several years, but they were wrong. Sales manager Arthur Davidson and his assistant, Albert Becker, recruited new dealers at a dizzying rate. Almost overnight, Harley-Davidson became a force in the marketplace. Production jumped from 150 in 1907 to 3,200 in 1910. Crating was done on the street. Even the old woodshed was pressed back into service.

The Harley-Davidson machine took hold quickly for several reasons. Foremost was the strong demand for a handsome and dependable mount. Advanced over much of the competition when prototyped in 1903, Harley kept ahead of the pack while others stuck to outmoded designs or shoddy construction. There was no radical revision needed, as was the case for Indian in 1909 when that company finally abandoned the bicycle frame.

Changes to the Harley-Davidson were cautious and made only to improve the original pattern.

Looking north on 38th Street toward Chestnut Street (now Juneau Avenue), new construction rises on the site of the yellow brick factory. Unless an early prototype, the bicycle is not a Harley-Davidson, as the Motor Company did not start selling bicycles until 1918 and this photo was taken in 1912. PHOTO COURTESY MILWAUKEE COUNTY HISTORICAL SOCIETY

By early 1911, an addition had been added to the first, five-story, red brick structure built in 1910. To its right, we see Harley's yellow brick factory and attached saw-tooth roof machine shop. In 1912–1913 new buildings would replace these quaint reminders of Harley's early years. *PHOTO COURTESY MILWAUKEE COUNTY HISTORICAL SOCIETY*

Upgrades came in 1907 with the Sager spring fork; in 1909 with increased displacement of 30.16 cubic inches (495 cc), magneto ignition, hidden controls, and restyled tanks; and in 1910 with an improved belt idler.

Just as vital was Harley-Davidson's commitment to its dealers—nearly 2,000 by 1916. The Milwaukee

As motorcycle production soared, new construction tried to keep pace. This late 1912 view shows the north side of the Harley factory as an addition partly fills in the gap between the 1910–1911 red brick building and the big 1912 "east" addition, barely visible on the far left. By this date, the only remaining segment of the yellow brick factory was the sawtooth machine shop, seen here displaying the large Harley-Davidson name. *PHOTO COURTESY MILWAUKEE COUNTY HISTORICAL SOCIETY*

Owned by the Harley Archives and on display at the Milwaukee Public Museum, this 1909 twin represents the rarest of the rare. Most writers incorrectly state that the 1909 twin was 49.48 cubic inches (810 cc), but displacement was actually 53.68 cubic inches (880 cc).

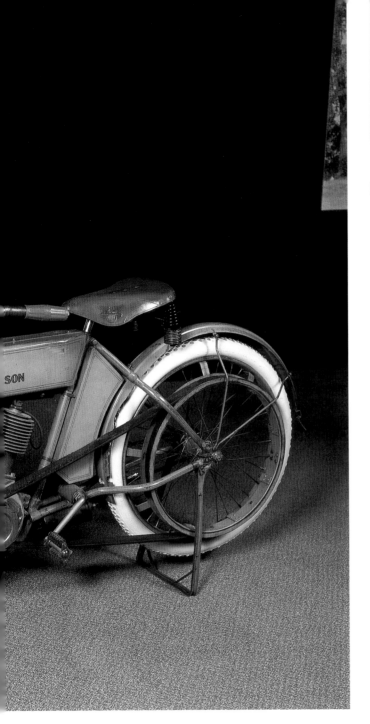

"Beehive"-style cylinders made pre-1911 twins unique. Some blamed the 1909 twin's failure on its lack of a belt tensioner, but H-D said the trouble was with the automatic intake valves. When the bike was new it would have run a 28-degree V-belt and not the flat belt shown here.

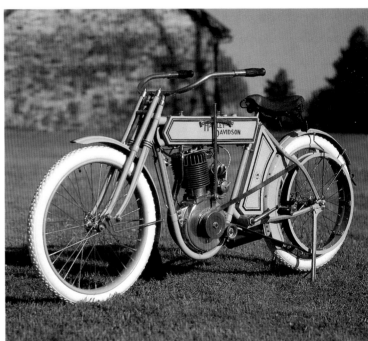

Chalmer Davidson's nicely restored 1911 magneto-equipped Model 7-C in a rustic setting evokes a less hurried past. By 1911, the Silent Gray Fellow was quickly gaining popularity among American riders.

The gear train on the 1911 magneto model was a major departure from that of earlier battery models. Vertical fins gave 1911 and later motors a different look, although little else had changed.

factory backed its already dependable product with high-quality parts and expert advice. Harley-Davidson president Walter Davidson's "1,000 plus 5" win of the country's premier endurance run in 1908 showed the world Harley-Davidson enthusiasm and durability. With Harley-Davidson, a dealer made both money and friends.

The founders of Harley-Davidson also made the canny decision to grow with the market. In early 1910, they laid the foundation of the modern company by purchasing land west of the yellow brick factory and erecting a new five-story structure of reinforced concrete and red brick.

The new plant was of modern industrial design and contained end walls of removable tiles for future expansion. This came immediately. In November a second red brick addition was authorized. Built on the west side of the new red brick plant, it was finished early in 1911.

Curiously, a story of a hidden room is associated with this second segment of the Juneau

Avenue factory. It tells of early bike parts used as backfill behind a wall in the basement. This was told to the author by the late Albert "Squib" Henrich, who in turn heard it from early employee Edwin "Sherbie" Becker in the early 1920s. An attempt in 1992 to find the hidden room proved inconclusive.

Legend aside, production in 1911 zoomed to over 5,600. This included several hundred of the new twin-cylinder models.

America's first V-twin had been marketed by future aviator Glenn Curtiss in 1903 when he introduced a 42.4-cubic-inch (695 cc), 5-horsepower twin. Two years later, in college, Bill Harley began doodling V-twin designs. A second cylinder added to the single was an easy path to more hill-climbing oomph.

Belts had to be kept clean and oiled, and the idler pulley "dropped" at night. When the belt had stretched beyond the limits of idler pulley travel, the rear wheel was moved back and a link added to the pedaling chain.

Owner-builder Bruce Linsday resurrected this 1911 twin around a bare engine. The frame was hand-built, and the rest of the machine is a combination of original and replica parts.

The first Harley-Davidson V-twin prototype was built in late 1906. In February 1907, it was shown at the Chicago motorcycle show. It was rated at 5 horsepower, but displacement and specs are unknown.

There is evidence that a few additional twins were built in 1907 and 1908 as prototypes or racers. A reported 27 twins were built in 1909, and at least one in 1910. The 1909 twin displaced 53.68 cubic inches (880 cc).

To illustrate the rarity of pre-1911 H-D twins, just one example appears in Wisconsin motorcycle registrations before 1911. This was a 7-horsepower 1909 "Model 5-D," registered that spring to H-D engine department foreman Max Kobs.

Everyone else at Harley was still riding singles—including the founders. Not until 1911 were additional twins registered. This was the redesigned 50-cubic-inch (810 cc) Model 7-D. In 1912, a 61-cubic-inch (988 cc) version appeared that soon nudged the smaller twin out of existence.

Harley-Davidson was now on a roll of epic proportions. Output exploded from 9,591 in 1912 to 16,000 in 1914. In 1913, a milestone was

According to Linsday, his early Harley twin isn't much faster than the single, but it goes up hills much better. The V-twin motor fills up the frame nicer too.

reached when more twins than singles were built.

This rapid increase sent Harley-Davidson motorcycles around the globe, a feat made possible by yet more enlargements to the Juneau Avenue plant.

In early 1912, the properties between the yellow brick factory and 37th Street were purchased and the buildings razed. Dynamite broke the frozen ground and Henry Wussow's steam shovel excavated earth that was hauled away by horse-drawn wagons. By May, the Meyer Construction Co. was pouring concrete. Experts were amazed at their speedy progress.

This "east" plant was Harley-Davidson's most ambitious addition during this period. The building was L-shaped to fit the wedge-shaped property and to allow natural light into the structure. Over 700 freight-car loads fed the concrete mixer, and 500,000 pounds of steel reinforcing rod were used. Meyer's crew ("Italian sculptors" Arthur Davidson called them in the Harley-Davidson *Dealer*) mixed, poured, and tamped 28 million pounds of concrete in just 75 days.

On the first of August the top floor was poured

Of his twin's performance, Linsday said, "You can slow down to about 15 miles per hour and then pull the belt tensioner. The belt chirps a couple times and you're off and up to 50 real nice."

Mike Terry's original-condition 1913 single features acetylene lighting, with the acetylene tank mounted on the handlebar. Night riding was a problem in the early days, and many deaths were attributable to hazardous roads and poor lighting.

After singing the praises of automatic intake valves for years, Harley-Davidson went to a mechanically operated intake valve on its single in 1913. This arrangement would remain unchanged until 1930.

Another option in 1913 was the chain-drive single, as shown on this H-D Archives bike at the Milwaukee Public Museum.

What appears to be a rear brake drum on this 1913 single is actually Bill Harley's Free Wheel Control. This modern multi-plate clutch device was a $10 option on both singles and twins. The Free Wheel Control lever is located behind the belt-tensioner lever.

and a Milwaukee German custom observed when a Christmas tree was hoisted aloft. This signaled company president Walter Davidson that Meyer's crew was entitled to free beer.

The east plant added 90,000 square feet of floor space to the factory, thereby doubling the capacity of all previous additions combined. The need for more production space was so great that machinery was installed on a floor as soon as Edward Steigerwald's brick masons closed it in.

But even this wasn't enough room. In September, offices were moved out of the yellow brick factory and a crew razed everything except the sawtooth machine shop. The *Dealer* noted, "The . . . first structure erected on the present site of the Harley-Davidson factory . . . has now passed into history."

With autumn closing in, work on the new addition continued day and night. Arnold Meyer promised "a floor a week" to an anxious Walter Davidson, who held out a $150-per-day bonus for an early finish.

Experts called them crazy for attempting two buildings in one season. As the structure rose, workers in the east building watched the Bar and Shield trademark on the west factory vanish behind the new construction. Good weather held and the latest addition was occupied as 1913 dawned.

The Motor Company now occupied a factory of nearly 200,000 square feet. With so many new additions, a numbering system was devised, starting with the original woodshed dubbed "factory number 1."

In 1913, the last gap along Juneau Avenue was closed when the 1909 machine shop was razed and was replaced by a six-story plant.

Again, Meyer's crew carried out its duties with precision. The "big bucket" tipped its first load of concrete in May and its last in July. By fall the addition was complete.

Thus, by 1914, Harley-Davidson possessed 300,000 square feet of capacity under one roof. The plant ran along Juneau Avenue for 476 feet. Experts declared the new factory perfect in every respect.

With partition walls removed, the various segments merged into a single facility as workers moved freely throughout the plant. The identities of additions Nos. 3, 4, 5, 6, and 8—along with the now vanished yellow brick factory—were soon forgotten.

The original woodshed was brought to the Juneau Avenue factory where it stood for decades as a reflection of the past. For in ten years' time a backyard operation had been transformed into a world-famous company.

The founders looked confidently toward the future, but other forces were at work: forces that would threaten everyone's lofty predictions.

CHAPTER 5
THE
FIGHTING MOTORCYCLE

World War I devastated the original U.S. motorcycle industry. In 1914, there were nearly two dozen factories turning out heavyweight V-twin motorcycles. Rising wages and prices, scarcity of components, and better profits elsewhere killed off the majority of builders. When the dust settled in 1919 you could count the survivors on one hand. But if the war wrecked the smaller concerns, it helped Harley-Davidson.

The U.S. Army first tested motorcycles in 1908, but found the iron horse wanting compared to the four-legged variety. By the time of World War I, however, the Harley-Davidson had grown up, as evidenced by the chart on page 40.

While the Harley-Davidson motorcycle of 1916 was a world apart from the 1905 model, an unbroken design continuity lay between these machines. Just as Bill Harley had "growed" the single into a twin by grafting on a second cylinder, further improvements were made in step-by-step increments until 1916 when the classic American motorcycle layout stabilized. It remained unchanged for the next 33 years.

By 1914, the War Department was testing motorcycles again, inspired this time by the mechanization of European armies. During World War I, the British Army alone used 70,000 bikes. A new and unexpected use for the motorcycle had come into being: warfare.

Technically neutral until 1917, the U.S. Army had no battle-ground experience with the motorcycle until 1916. Then trouble developed along the Mexican border with Pancho Villa's revolutionary army. This gave Harley-Davidson an excuse for taking the motorcycle into the fight.

Some National Guard units had already formed motorcycle companies. One Illinois H-D dealer was begging the government for machine guns so his riders could act as "light artillery." Wanting something official, the U.S. Army invited Bill Harley to the Springfield Armory where he helped develop the "fighting motorcycle."

The military had high hopes for the new weapon. Unlike the mule-packed machine gun that took several minutes to unload and set up, the sidecar machine gun was available within seconds. Some claimed a single machine-gun-equipped sidecar equaled 1,000 riflemen in firepower!

> ## "This is no place for a timid person like me."
> —Arthur Davidson on the Mexican border, 1916

This 1916 twin located in H-D Archives, shows the great advance the Silent Gray Fellow made in 10 years' time. This is the bike H-D took to war. Building seen through window is the "Factory No. 5" portion of the Juneau Avenue complex built in 1912.

With the adoption of the kickstarter in 1916, the modern H-D layout stabilized. In 1915, they had a three-speed transmission but with "step" starting, and in 1914, a two-speed rear hub with pedal starting. Before that, it was all single-speed.

1905 H-D, Single Cylinder
Displacement: 26.84 cubic inches (440 cc)
Output: 3 1/4 horsepower
Ignition: coil/dry-cell battery
Lubrication: drip feed
Suspension: front: rigid, rear: seat springs
Transmission: none (single speed)
Starting: jump on/no clutch
Wheelbase: 51 inches
Tires: 2 1/4 inches
Final drive: flat belt
Weight: 138 pounds
Lighting: none
Top speed: 50 miles per hour (racing pulley)

1916 H-D, Twin Cylinder
Displacement: 60.34 cubic inches (988.83 cc)
Output: 11 horsepower
Ignition: magneto or generator-battery
Lubrication: pressurized feed-pump plus
    auxiliary handpump
Suspension: front: spring fork, rear: Ful-Floteing
    seat-post plus seat springs
Transmission: three-speed
Starting: kickstarter with clutch
Wheelbase: 59 1/2 inches
Tires: 3 inches
Final drive: chain
Weight: 325 pounds
Lighting: electric on Model 16-J
Top speed: 70 miles per hour

The fighting motorcycle was tested near Milwaukee, in deep mud, early in 1916. Firing at ranges between 250 and 500 yards, it satisfied military and factory observers. Afterwards, these machines were shipped to New Mexico for service along the border.

Propaganda dispatches from England portrayed the military motorcyclist as a romantic figure dodging mortar shells and machine gun fire. Riders were shown aiming a pistol in one direction while heading in another—a practice not conducive to longevity.

Early reports from Mexico told similar tales. One extolled Private Gregg of the U.S. Seventh Cavalry, who rode his Harley-Davidson through a gang of banditos with his .45 Colt semi-automatic pistol blazing, killing one, wounding another, then delivering his dispatch case safely at headquarters.

While such exciting events no doubt took place, the truth was closer to the report of one newspaper correspondent who wrote: "A motorcycle coughed past, chasing runaway mules through the mesquite."

Used against a lightly armed adversary on foot or horseback in the open Southwest, the machine-gun sidecar was probably fairly effective. Even so, hidden opponents armed with the accurate, clip-fed Mexican Mauser rifle could wreak havoc on a target as big as a sidecar.

Harley-Davidson's fighting motorcycle was tested in the spring of 1916 at a rifle range near the Racine-Milwaukee county line. Clay mud encountered en route forced the removal of the front fenders. After posing for photographers and being cleaned up at the factory, these machines were shipped to the Mexican border for active duty. PHOTO COURTESY MILWAUKEE COUNTY HISTORICAL SOCIETY

One thing quickly learned was the need to adequately train motorcyclist soldiers. Studies showed that 90 percent of a motorcycle's efficiency depended on the rider and mechanic and only 10 percent on the machine.

Badly trained conscripts were accident prone, and poorly maintained machines subject to breakdown. This moved the Milwaukee factory to send out instructors for training rider-soldiers and mechanics. A school at the factory was set up by service department head Joe Kilbert in 1917. Howard "Hap" Jameson was the first instructor. The service school exists to the present day.

Based on experience in Mexico, the Army forged ahead with the fighting motorcycle once officially engaged in the European conflict. Experts forecasted 20,000 motorcycles for every million soldiers in the trenches.

The reality of modern warfare, however, was far different from skirmishing in Mexico. Bad ground, bottomless mud, shattered roads, endless debris, booby traps, and vulnerability to return fire restricted the military motorcycle to rear-echelon service.

Here the motorcycle—usually with sidecar—did quite well for dispatch work, convoy control, military police, supply needs, communications repair, medic duty, and other auxiliary uses.

Still, wartime conditions demanded great durability. Even taking into account the self-congratulatory approach that Harley-Davidson was so good at, it appears that American machines stood up better in warfare than did English and French bikes—with Harleys doing best of all.

A special magazine—*Harley-Davidson Folks*—was published for servicemen. In late 1917, one soldier wrote to this publication: "for real comedy you ought to see . . . these French machines . . . so many levers and controls on them they look more like a linotype machine. . . . I actually had the nerve to . . . ride one, but got the spark to exploding in the transmission case and the exhaust snorted into the magneto and quit."

One Harley-Davidson reportedly took part in the Mexican border ruckus, then served in France on "16,000 miles of as rough a run as pneumatic tires have ever turned upon or engine pumped across."

This reputation led to the selection of William S. Harley as head of the Society of Automotive

Machine gun–equipped Harleys were given a thorough workout in the Southwest desert in 1916 as a prelude to their use in Europe. While shown here as mobile units of war able to run rings around an opponent, the combat role of the motorcycle turned out to be very limited. PHOTO COURTESY MILWAUKEE COUNTY HISTORICAL SOCIETY

This Milwaukee street scene was photographed shortly after America's entry into World War I. It suggests a Harley-Davidson rider has dismounted to hear the patriotic speech of an army recruiter. In total, 312 Harley-Davidson employees served in the armed forces. Three were killed. *PHOTO COURTESY MILWAUKEE COUNTY HISTORICAL SOCIETY*

Engineers' committee on standardized military motorcycles. Committee members came from the ranks of American motorcycle builders. Their work resulted in the "Liberty Motorcycle," a standardized machine based on the best features of various civilian types.

Harley-Davidson's major contributions included engine, wheels, and controls. Prototypes were built and tested in 1918, but the war ended before production began.

During the war, 312 employees from Harley-Davidson served in the armed forces. Three were killed in action.

Because Milwaukee was heavily German, American patriotism was serious business in Beer City. The bronze statue goddess *Germania* was cut up for scrap. A legend in the Harley family tells of government agents watching the house during the war because Bill Harley's wife, Anna, was of German descent. On the day of the armistice, Harley-Davidson employees led the victory parade downtown.

The war boosted Harley-Davidson in several ways. Unlike Indian, who early-on took big military contracts, the Milwaukee factory did not commit to full war production until very late. Dealers could get bikes and parts from Harley all through the war except for a six-month period in 1918.

As a result, disgruntled Indian riders and orphans from the many now-defunct makes swelled Harley's ranks. Harley-Davidson could brag about not diverting production into the foreign military market as Indian had—thus portraying Milwaukee as the rider's friend.

World War I gained Harley-Davidson a world-wide reputation for durability. In 1990, the late William H. Davidson told me, "Harley got its deepest breath over in the mud in France. . . . After World War I we went ahead of Indian and stayed ahead forever."

The greatest tribute to the Harley-Davidson motorcycle came after the war when surplus machines were sold at auction. After the new, still-in-the-crate

This 1919 J model, owned by John Vandenover, is similar to WWI Army bikes. Even the paint color is the same, although tank graphics on military bikes were less flamboyant.

Harleys were purchased, bidding agents from foreign governments announced they would buy *used* Harley-Davidsons before buying new machines from other manufacturers.

Stories of World War I military Harleys still surface. One old-time Wisconsin rider, Alfred Embretsen, told me a story of a guy doing backhoe work years ago at Camp McCoy, where in 1917 the Milwaukee Motorcycle Ambulance Co. No. 1 was stationed.

"He dug up an entire row of World War I Harleys," Embretsen said. "Some were still in the crates. There were horse saddles and other equipment too. When he asked if he could salvage them, the officer in charge hollered, 'Nothing doing! Go back out there and bury them right back up.'"

CHAPTER 6
THE
GANG'S ALL HERE

After World War I the American motorcycling landscape was drastically altered. Great names had vanished forever. Indian now occupied second place, and Ignaz Schwinn's Excelsior-Henderson brought up the rear.

Milwaukee was on top.

At Harley-Davidson the old guard was firmly in place. Founders William S. Harley, Arthur Davidson, Walter Davidson, and William A. Davidson were now in their prime.

Several top men had followed Bill Davidson from the railshops, including plant supervisor George Nortman. Other valuable employees had come from the Thor and Feilbach motorcycle companies.

An efficient office and sales staff; experienced engineering, experimental, and racing departments; and hundreds of skilled machinists and laborers rounded out the work force at Harley-Davidson,

"For the rider who simply must have the fastest thing on wheels."
—Two-Cam sales literature, 1928

which totaled 2,350 people in a company that had done $14 million of business in 1919 dollars.

With the prewar competition weeded out and greater dealer and rider loyalty in place, the good times seemed ready to roll. Once again, Harley-Davidson expanded. In 1919, the new "south" complex at Juneau Avenue was begun. Factory floor space again doubled, with production capacity rising to 35,000 motorcycles per year—a figure the founders would never see reached.

The peak year for the American motorcycle industry was 1913. As shown, the war was a double-edged sword—helping Harley-Davidson but knocking out many smaller outfits. After 1920, however, even Milwaukee was feeling pain, no matter how hard they tried to ignore it. This reversal in fortunes was largely due to Henry Ford's Model T.

Reliable and cheap to begin with, the Model T just kept getting cheaper. By the 1920s the motorcycle's early popularity had vanished. The time when doctors used two-wheelers for house calls was gone forever.

The motorcycle's early price advantage was also gone. A cost comparison between Harley's V-twin

Although Clifford Pease's restored 1922 JD model is not completely authentic, it's still a good example of an early 74-cubic-inch Harley F-head. By 1922, Ford's Model T had dropped below the Harley Big Twin in price.

and Ford's Model T illustrates the throat-slashing competition the motorcycle faced:

Harley-Davidson (Twin)	Ford Model T (Runabout)
1909 (54 ci) $325	1909 $825
1913 (61 ci) $350	1913 $525
1916 (61 ci) $295	1916 $345
1920 (61 ci) $395	1920 (March) $550
	(Sept.) $395
1922 (74 ci) $390	1922 $319
1925 (74 ci) $335	1925 $260

Ford's downward pressure on the price of transportation was crushing. After 1920, Ford's cheapest car actually dropped *below* Harley's V-twin in price. Historians who beat the tom-tom of an "Indian vs. Harley" war have it wrong. That was nothing but a sideshow to excite the riders. Behind the scenes, Harley-Davidson, "Pop" Schwinn, and Indian worked together. They knew the real enemy—Henry Ford.

Without the economy of scale that Ford possessed, no motorcycle factory could compete on a price basis. At the 1920 dealers' convention, a bitter Walter Davidson said, "Henry Ford is given credit for the price decline [but] he simply is a victim of circumstances. . . . His car will carry you over the road, but has none of the qualifications that a modern car has."

This was whistling in the graveyard, and Walter knew it. The motorcycle was in deep trouble. The Ford wasn't fancy, but as basic transportation it had more "qualifications" than any motorcycle. To approximate an automobile you needed a sidecar, and that cost another hundred bucks.

Attempting to broaden the motorcycle's appeal, Harley-Davidson introduced the "Sport Model" (Model W) in 1919. This 35.64-cubic-inch (584 cc) "flat twin" showed some advanced and original features. If patents granted to Bill Harley are any indication, Milwaukee had big plans for it.

It's tempting to say that the Sport Model was intended to be a two-wheeled Model T. It weighed a hundred pounds less than the V-twin, and, with its low center of gravity, was a sweet handling mount. Its opposed-cylinder engine was sewing-machine smooth, and with gear primary-drive and enclosed rear chain it was quiet, clean, and efficient.

In theory, the public should have flocked to the Sport, but like most smaller motorcycles that appeared in the post–World War I period, it failed. Price was one barrier—$325 in 1919. There was also the Sport's unorthodox appearance, which damned it in the eyes of V-twin–loving Americans. Weak performance was another nail in the Sport's coffin. After five years it faded away, leaving the 61-cubic-inch V-twin to carry the torch, along with the 74-cubic-inch "Superpowered Twin" that appeared in 1921.

Intended for sidecar and high-speed solo work, the 74 was a 61 that had been bored and stroked

Standard J-series engine used a single camshaft with cam followers that severely limited rpm, but that was not so important in an age of poor roads and 30-mile-per-hour speed limits.

46

Harley's Sport Model was unorthodox with its opposed horizontal cylinders and external flywheel. Almost nothing on it followed standard Harley practice. Bob McClean own's this nice 1922 example.

to 3 7/16x4 inches. Harley-Davidson knew its customers' tastes when advertising that. "If you want to enjoy the feel and thrill of piloting a motorcycle of extra mighty power, get a Harley-Davidson 74 Superpowered Twin Motorcycle."

From the beginning the motorcycle had been defined by speed and power, but that too came back to haunt Harley-Davidson. Because if Milwaukee wasn't busy enough fighting the cheap automobile, there was another problem to battle: the public's hatred for two-wheelers.

Guess again if you think the "bad boy" image started with *The Wild One*. In the beginning the masses despised *all* motor vehicles. But while the automobile became acceptable, the motorcycle industry nearly committed *hara-kiri* by exploiting the two-wheeler's most troubling aspect: sudden death.

The emphasis on speed racing came from the motorcycle's bicycle roots. The biggest early racing promoter was a former bicycle racing champ—Indian founder George Hendee.

The Sport Model engine was Harley's first side-valve. Transmission was positioned over the engine. Note the combined intake and exhaust manifolds.

Hendee used the Indian motorcycle like a war club. He encouraged dealers to race and sent factory teams on the warpath to scalp the competition. Under Hendee, Indian reigned supreme.

In the day of the single-cylinder this didn't mean much, but with the rise of the V-twin and track speeds of 100 miles per hour by 1912 on the wooden-banked motordromes, the motorcycle's homicidal soul was released.

Board-track racing was dubbed the "craziest sport in the world" by newspapers, which decorated motordrome articles with grim reapers and winged death's heads. Outraged by the infernal racket of unmuffled engines and the aura of violent death, the public labeled them "murder-dromes" and civic do-gooders demanded their abolition.

Harley-Davidson long resisted this racing trend. Their motorcycle was of a practical nature—

Harley's Eight-Valve racer bested Indian in the 1910s and 1920s, but professional racing, with its many deaths and injuries, put a black mark on the sport of motorcycling. John Paeham's excellent 1928 model was "built" by Mike Lange.

Close-up of a 1927 Eight-Valve engine shows the large dual exhaust ports and multi-valve arrangement. This was Harley's only four-valve-per-head engine until the VR1000 factory racer appeared in 1994. Motor courtesy R. L. Jones.

The Harley F-head went out in a blaze of glory with the 1928 Two-Cam road model. Acceleration was brisk with a top solo speed of about 80 to 85 miles per hour. Mike Terry owns this nice 74-cubic-inch JDH.

a dependable pleasure mount where high speed was not an end in itself. For the first decade this formula proved successful. When the factory competed they favored endurance and reliability events, and except for a few attempts early on, shied away from pure speed.

This changed in 1912 when a motordrome was built in Milwaukee. The roar of racing victories could be heard all over town, but none went to the home factory. The laughing Indian appeared on billboards and everybody knew the butt of the joke: Harley-Davidson.

Enough was enough. In 1913, Harley-Davidson enticed racing boss William Ottaway away from Thor—the god of thunder. Of Ottaway, the late William H. Davidson said, "[He] developed the first Eight-Valve and the standard pocket-valve [racers]. . . . He got those so they would sing . . . a fine mechanical wizard."

After a mediocre start in 1914, the Harley-Davidson factory team—soon dubbed the "wrecking crew"—took sweeping victories at Dodge City and other prestigious events. With the famous Two-Cam and Eight-Valve racers, Harley-Davidson smashed Indian's former dominance into pieces that the once-proud "Wigwam" could never put back together again.

But speed racing came with a heavy price. Advertising manager Walter Kleimenhagen told dealers, "racing—that magic form of advertising . . . it's great . . . but land sakes how it costs."

The price went beyond dollars and cents. It gave the motorcycle a deadly image and stereotyped the rider as an antisocial speed freak—a maniac dashing from place to place with throttle and cut-out wide open. spilling his guts over the landscape in the process.

It's ironic that today, an important part of Harley-Davidson marketing is based on a "bad boy" image. because for much of the company's history such an idea was taboo. Yet the founders themselves were responsible for this state of affairs when they turned their plow horse into a racing stud.

In 1928, they caved in to this lust for speed by offering the previously competition-only Two-Cam engine in road-bike form. These were the famous JH (61-cubic-inch) and JDH (74-cubic-inch) models. At the time, these bikes were the fastest stock Harleys ever offered and among the fastest vehicles on the road. In one ad a factory oracle said. "The magic words 'two cam' mean exceptional speed and tremendous power."

This shows how schizophrenic Harley-Davidson could be. Time and again they'd swear off racing and decry speed. but then like addicts they'd come crawling back to the race track or encourage road riders with the Two-Cam. In 1929, you could even special order an 80-cubic-inch Two-Cammer!

Together these poisoned apple factors removed the American motorcycle from mainstream transportation into a suspect. cult-like status. Throughout the 1920s. H-D operated at about half capacity. Export. commercial. and law enforcement sales kept the factory alive. but the motorcycle found itself in dark waters. with civic reformers asking why it should exist at all.

Front wheel brake first appeared in 1928 and wasn't the dangerous device many thought. By the late 1920s, however, the Big Twin was taking on an antiquated look. Few significant changes had taken place for several years.

CHAPTER 7

SINGLES FOR THE MASSES

But speed was just one card in Harley's deck. More typically, the company portrayed the sidecar as an elegant alternative to the auto-mobile. Colorful ads showed finely coiffured ladies disembarking at theaters or restaurants.

Another tactic had overseas origins. From their "London branch," H-D's founders were familiar with the English bike scene. They marveled at the clean reputation motor-cycles possessed in Great Britain, where all ages and classes rode.

This inspired Harley's "good rider" campaign. Ads offered "English serge" outfits, and slogans such as "Natty Suits for Neat Riders." During the 1920s, British tweeds were high motorcycle fash-ion. Accessory manager Hugh Sharp commented to dealers in 1920, "The sight of the white-col-lared chap with . . . neat fitting clothing and quiet running motorcycle is a creator of envy . . . instead of being a disturber of mental machinery."

"The overhead Singles were not without friends."
—New York Motorcycle Show, 1928

In 1926, attempting to create a more socially acceptable bike that would also appeal to the export market, Harley-Davidson introduced a new machine: the Model B 21-cubic-inch Single.

With 2 7/8 x 3 1/4-inch bore and stroke, the new Single displaced just 21.09 cubic inches (350 cc). It was the smallest Harley-Davidson to date—smaller than the original 405 cc 1903 bike.

Taking into account their experience with the innovative but unconventional Sport Model, H-D built the new Single along traditional lines. In the United States it was aimed at riders intimidated by the Big Twin, and also provided a low-cost alternative to the automobile.

Overseas, where gasoline prices were higher, the factory hoped that the Single's great econ-omy, along with Harley-Davidson reliability, would translate into big sales—and profits.

Tipping the scales at around 260 pounds, the new Single was no lightweight. Hap Jameson said in the *Enthusiast*, "When my turn came to try out this new member of the family I kinda felt like I had been asked to go strolling a baby cart. But, that little boat is no baby cart—no siree."

The 21 Single is usually lost in the stampede of V-twins, when in truth it was a landmark bike

The 1926 Model B was Harley's first 21-cubic-inch Sin-gle. This machine was a test bed for several new fea-tures and developed into the side-valve twins. Its spring fork is similar to that used on the 1936 Knucklehead. Owned by Don Huffman and Greg Taylor.

because with it, Bill Harley was mapping the future.

Using a twin-cam layout, the new Single was a smaller motorcycle with a big-bike ancestry and look. It ran full-sized footboards, a pressurized oil system, and a three-speed transmission. Electrics were the same as the Big Twin's. "Just like its papa," Hap boasted proudly, handing out verbal cigars to potential buyers.

The fork was new, and similar in style to 1936-and-later springers. The frame was a lighter version of the Big Twin's with the same spring seatpost. "No jolting . . . your gold fillings when you ride this baby," Hap promised.

Balloon tires improved the ride even more. "Hot puppies," Hap exclaimed. "These big rubber doughnuts are comfort producers."

Styling of the new Single followed the "streamline" look that first appeared on 1925 Big

The 21 Single was dubbed an "80 miles per gallon" bike due to great economy of operation.

Both the 45 and the Sportster inherited their right-side drive chain position from the 21 Single. The bearing bosses for the two camshafts are clearly evident from embossing on cover. The first 45 was this bike with a second cylinder and two more cams thrown in.

Twins. With shapely tanks and a lower frame, the modern Harley look was ushered in.

But the real significance of the Single was its existence in two similar, yet radically different, forms. You might call them rival fraternal twins because the Model "B" had a side-valve engine, while the Model BA had an overhead-valve engine.

The side-valve Single was no great shakes. That engine type had been championed by Indian for years and Harley had used it in the Sport Model. But the BA—the 21 OHV Single—was another story.

Except for professional Eight-Valve overhead racers, Harley riders had never seen an overhead-valve engine come out of Milwaukee. Now they had one in road-bike form—if only a single.

Already in the 1910s, riders knew that putting overhead valves in the gasoline engine was a kick-ass

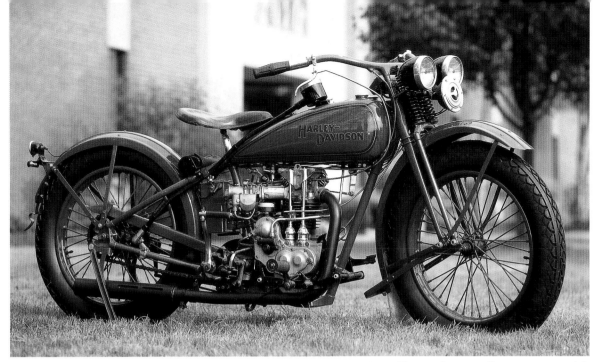

With front stand and foot pegs, this 21 OHV at the AMA's Motorcycle Heritage Museum is set up like an export model. Dual headlights are probably not original.

combination. It was still heady stuff in 1926 when the BA hit the street with its pushrod-activated valves opening into a hemispherical-shaped combustion chamber. This was the kind of technology you'd find in high-performance aircraft engines.

Logically, Harley-Davidson should have trumpeted the BA's superior overhead-valve technology from the lofty ramparts of Juneau Avenue. Curiously, they did not. Milwaukee was strangely silent about the 21 OHV. When presenting the 1926 line in the *Enthusiast*, the 21 OHV version was missing—an eerie foreshadowing of the 61 OHV's stealth introduction 10 years later.

Harley-Davidson probably chose not to push the 21 OHV because H-D's next generation of V-twins were all going to be side-valves. The first, the 45-cubic-inch (2 3/4x3 13/16-inch bore and stroke) Model D V-twin was introduced in 1929. The D was little more than the side-valve 21 Single

The 21 OHV was a small masterpiece of overhead-valve engineering. Combustion chamber shape and rocker arm design would find their way into the legendary Knucklehead engine.

Exposed valve springs look archaic to modern eyes. Serial number BA3010 suggests a first year 21 OHV, as 1926 and 1927 Singles did not have the year prefix in the serial number. Numbers began at 1000 in 1926 and at 9000 in 1927.

Thus, it wouldn't pay to sing hosannas to the overhead-valve Single when the new twins were all side-valves. The 21 OHV was like Cinderella locked in the attic while her side-valve sisters were portrayed as technological beauty queens with their "famous Ricardo Combustion Heads."

That was true—sort of. Harry Ricardo had breathed new life into the side-valve engine by redesigning the shape of the combustion chamber. This permitted higher compression with less chance of detonation. ("Whew!" Hap groaned in the *Enthusiast*. "I wish engineers would use words that mean something to me.")

with a second cylinder and two more cams incorporated into the motor. At first the 45 and 21 even shared frame and transmission.

In 1930, the new Model VL 74-cubic-inch side-valve Big Twin joined the lineup. Harley bragged that the VL was essentially an enlarged 45 twin. Not very exciting stuff. Lots of guys stuck with their Two-Cams.

Economics probably tipped Harley's hand. Cheap to build, the side-valve would pay the bills. In the automobile industry, the side-valve engine dominated; Harley-Davidson was just joining the party.

But there were plenty of people around Harley-Davidson who considered the side-valve to be Indian's motor and hated it. Alfred Feldmann, then in H-D's engineering department, later recalled of the side-valve in Maurice Hendry's 1972 book *Harley-Davidson*, "I was never in favor of that valve arrangement in an air-cooled engine."

The 45-cubic-inch side-valve engine appeared in 1929 as an answer to the Super X and Indian Scout. Note that each valve has its own camshaft and a very straight valve angle. Bob and Patti Studer own this 1932 Servi-Car.

The VL side-valve 74-cubic-inch engine replaced the F-head in the Big Twin line in 1930. It was little more than an enlarged 45. The Bluegrass Motorcycle Museum in Kentucky owns this handsome example.

While the side-valve engine was a cleaner design than its F-head predecessors, road conditions and rider expectations were racing ahead of the performance the VL could deliver.

As a result, most 21 Singles were side-valves. This was the famous "80 miles per gallon" bike, so cheap to run it would have pleased the Scots "honey uncle." As Hap promised, "The hinges on your old pocket book will rust from non-use if you buy gas for this buggy."

At last Harley-Davidson had a Model T on two wheels. The Single was cheaper to operate than an auto (1 cent per mile vs. 7 cents), cheaper than streetcar fare, and easy to park. The Single was billed as the new way to "power travel" that you could purchase with easy "Pay As You Ride" terms.

The 21 Single even undercut Ford's cheapest car by $150; trouble was, nobody much cared anymore. Used autos glutted the market. After a good production start of 8,000 in 1926, numbers started falling off. This decline was largely the result of Harley's export market drying up due to a stiff rise in British tariff rates throughout the "sterling bloc."

In this country, H-D made the mistake of targeting the Single to automobile drivers when the real market was boys and teenagers. One critic wrote to Arthur Davidson in 1927, "I am for the motorcyclist and not for the automobile owner." Under these circumstances the poor little Single never had a chance.

Yet all was not lost. In 1925, the American Motorcycle Association (AMA) sanctioned a new 21.35-cubic-inch racing class. The inaugural race was held in Milwaukee with a crowd of 20,000 watching Eddie Brinck, Jim Davis, and Joe Petrali sling their wicked little Singles around the track, cracking 80 miles per hour on the straight. This was the dawn of Harley's famous "Peashooter."

Anyone wandering down for a look at the racing bikes quickly had their eyes opened. For all the Peashooters had overhead-valve engines—a high performance version of the 21 OHV road bike.

The VL was an interesting bike during a transition period in Harley history. While reminiscent of earlier bikes in many ways, the VL was a more substantial machine. Hand oil pump is visible just behind left-hand filler caps.

Competition 21 Singles were overhead-valve, as shown on this 1926 example owned by Bruce Linsday. These little bikes could easily crack 80 miles per hour.

The overhead-valve Peashooter gave Harley lots of valuable experience on the racetrack. This was Harley's first engine with a hemispherical combustion chamber.

Word soon leaked out. Even the editor of the *Enthusiast* (as politically correct then as now) cryptically remarked. "The old timers, the vet riders after witnessing these 21 cubic inch races agreed that the future of motorcycle racing in America depends largely upon them."

For no matter how much brag was given to genuine Ricardo heads or 80 miles-per-gallon, astute parties could see the 21 OHV was a hot little number. The Peashooter was Harley's bright spot on the racetrack during the late 1920s and showed the way ahead. From this small beginning, the words "overhead-valve" soon became a mantra for performance-minded riders.

Yet anyone wishing for an overhead-valve twin from Milwaukee was greatly disappointed with the new 45- and 74-cubic-inch side-valve twins. An overhead-valve road twin from Harley-Davidson probably seemed as far away as the moon.

HOME-BREW
AND FACTORY 45 OHVs

In reality, new Harley-Davidson overhead-valve twins were not far away, but when they appeared in 1927 they weren't factory jobs, but radical homebuilt hillclimbers.

By the mid-1920s, the hillclimber had eclipsed the motorcycle speed artist. As the club scene grew under the auspices of the AMA, so did slant shooting. All a club needed was a steep country slope where roaring motorcycles weren't a social contagion.

Professional riders ruled the slant. Factory or dealer provided a hillclimb bike, mechanic, and travel expenses. The rider provided the skill and kept the winnings. Slant artists were considered *real* men and were popular with the ladies.

> "It's a pleasure to see Art ride but the girls get a bigger 'goose flesh' out of his 'smile.' These motorcycle boys DO get 'em."
> —*The Harley-Davidson Enthusiast*

Although hillclimbing was rough and tumble, serious injuries were rare. Image-sensitive Harley-Davidson liked that. But winning was everything, and while H-D's 61- and 80-cubic-inch F-head hillclimbers were competitive in the larger displacement events, Milwaukee was caught short in the hot new 45-cubic-inch class.

Back in 1925, Chicago-based Excelsior-Henderson threw a wild card into the mix with their new 45-cubic-inch Super X twin. This F-head sported advanced features, which included gear primary-drive and strong unit construction.

In this trend toward smaller, higher performance motorcycles, the 45 class quickly became an arena for the pros. On the Super X, Joe Petrali and Gene Rhyne reclaimed Excelsior's early glory by winning several hillclimb championships.

Indian countered the Super X threat by enlarging its Scout to 45 cubic inches in 1927, and later dished out more-potent 45 OHV hillclimbers. Until

The engine in this hillclimber is the 1928 hybrid Two-Cam/OHV. It has a JDH bottom end, Peashooter heads, and special cast cylinders. The bike is owned by the Motorcycle Heritage Museum and is on display at the Motorsports Hall of Fame Museum.

1929, Harley-Davidson was the underdog in the 45 class. Without a 45-cubic-inch hillclimber, Harley riders played catch up as they hollered at Milwaukee for help.

Significantly, the 21 OHV Single was sometimes effective in battling Super X and Indian 45s.

It happened in 1926, when Herb Reiber's win at Slinger, Wisconsin, allowed the *Enthusiast* to crow, "The . . . Single slipped a fast one over when it assailed the slant in the 45 . . . Event, leaving the twins to take second and third. Wow! A Single beats twins!"

Motor in the Two-Cam/OHV was done so professionally by H-D's experimental and racing departments that it's difficult to see it's actually two engines combined into one. Until now, the Two-Cam/OHV's key role in Harley history has been overlooked.

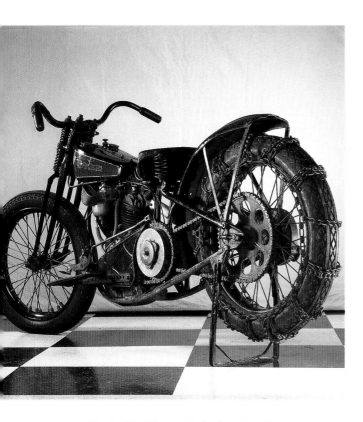

The business end of the Two-Cam/OHV shows the reason for an overhead-valve hillclimb twin. Torque and high revs of this experimental 45 OHV provided a temporary solution in 1928 against Super X and Indian in the 45-cubic-inch class.

"made from two overhead-valve Singles." The Camel was good enough for Lenz to take some firsts in 1927 and 1928. The bike still exists.

Lenz's home-built 45 OHV Harley wasn't the only one active in 1927. In July, one observer noted a "new design Harley 42 [*sic*] cubic inch motor" built by Ralph Moore of Indianapolis. He added, "No, we did not hit the bottle or pick up a pipe before we wrote that last line. It is a fact. Moore took a 61 Harley, junked most of the motor except the cases, and constructed a 42 cubic inch Harley, using the cylinders and pistons from two 21 cubic inch O. V. Single Harleys."

Such David vs. Goliath victories were rare, and confined to hills that didn't need the chains and dig-out power necessary in loose dirt. But they made Harley riders gaze fondly at the high-revving Peashooter engine to see where the answer lay: overhead-valves.

Over the winter of 1926–1927, two enterprising Harley-Davidson dealers created 45 OHVs. These "Home-Brews" (named after a favorite Prohibition beverage) first appeared in June 1927, at a Lansing, Michigan, climb when Jack Pine enduro winner Oscar Lenz fielded a bike that *MotorCycling* described as a "45 cubic inch Harley" and onlookers dubbed "the Camel."

Lenz's Harley 45 was built on a 1925 61-cubic-inch Two-Cam bottom end with a top end

The frame on the Two-Cam/OHV appears to be from a later DAH factory hillclimber. The single-exhaust-port head differs from two other known Two-Cam/OHVs which have two-port heads, showing that Harley was experimenting.

This "built" 1930 DAH factory hillclimber was crafted by R. L. Jones. Hillclimber styling was the original inspiration for "bobber" and "chopper" road bikes. Note the original chopper-esque fuel tank and cool trailing-link fork.

Noting the success of the Lenz and Moore Home-Brews, Milwaukee created its own 45 OHV in 1928. Whether the impetus came from the Harley factory or Bill Knuth's nearby Milwaukee dealership isn't clear. Knuth promoted professional hillclimbing heavily, and was a factory pet. Although Harley was working on a totally new 45 OHV hillclimber (the 4-camshaft DAH), the factory had good reason to help Knuth. The DAH wouldn't be ready until 1929, and the pros were crying for a 45 OHV for the 1928 season.

Because the 1928 45 OHV hillclimber was not catalogued, determining the bike's origin is difficult. Documentation was lost when Harley-Davidson purged old records, after Bill Knuth's death in 1959.

It's unclear whether these experimental overheads were constructed at the factory or at Knuth's dealership. But if built by Knuth, there was certainly critical factory help. Old-timers remember Harley's experimental and racing departments giving "our Bill" anything he wanted.

Three of these unique 45 OHV hillclimbers survive. All are built on 1928 or 1929 FH or JDH Two-Cam crankcases and show evidence of being constructed by the same hands. Information from the Motorcycle Heritage Museum tells that paid-factory-hillclimber and assistant-service-school-instructor Herb Reiber reworked patterns for the 21 Single cylinder from which six pairs of new cylinders were cast to fit the bigger Two-Cam bottom end.

Due to the excellent workmanship evident on the surviving engines, it's likely that Harley's experimental department reworked the 21 OHV heads to make front and rear cylinders for a twin. Antique bike restorer Mike Lange, who worked on one of these hybrid motors, said this about the cylinder head modifications he noted. "The intake manifold was done up very professionally with a nickel (welding) rod. . . . Along with the cylinders it's my opinion that these were done at the factory."

The parent 61 motor's 3 1/2-inch stroke was retained while the bore was changed to 2 7/8 inches using the Dow metal Peashooter piston. This gave an engine of 45.44 cubic inches (744.6 cc) displacement. The resulting motor had the direct-cam action and strong internals of the Two-Cam racer with the breathing advantages of overhead-valves. By a quirk of fate, this experimental and largely forgotten 45 OHV hillclimber may have inspired the greatest motorcycle of them all: the Knucklehead.

The first appearance of Milwaukee's Two-Cam/OHV came in May of 1928—a full year before historians say H-D fielded a 45 OHV hill-climber. It was ridden at Fond du Lac, Wisconsin, by Art Earlenbaugh, who worked at Bill Knuth's dealership and later in H-D's experimental department. Correspondent Hap Jameson commented,

Redesigned Peashooter heads led to the DAH pattern. During the late 1920s and early 1930s, H-D experimented with OHV technology. One entire bike—the 1929 FAR, a 61-cubic-inch OHV export road racer—leaves no trace in the historical record.

A second "built" 1930 DAH by R. L. Jones nears completion. The author usually shies away from comparing motorcycles to works of art, but this example comes pretty close. Talent at H-D reached a peak in the 1930s.

"Earlenbaugh deserves a lot of credit because he made a good showing with his home-made 45."

A second bike was in the running by June, when Herb Reiber set a new AMA record piloting a 45 OHV twin. In July, it was observed at Dayton that "Herb Reiber, the Lone Star from Wisconsin, (was) riding one of those 'home brew' 45 Harleys." At Muskegon, Earlenbaugh and Moore competed on "homemade 45-inch jobs." Earlenbaugh took second place. Describing his bike, *MotorCycling* said, "The Milwaukee sheik . . . was sporting his own home brew two-port Harley job, a neat outfit and a real display of engineering skill. Herb Reiber also sports a job like Earlenbaugh's."

In August, the *Enthusiast* admitted something new was in the wind when reporting on the New Munster, Wisconsin, hillclimb: "All kinds of shooting irons were on the slant. Some 'Home-Brew' 45's and some that weren't home brew. . . . Art Earlenbaugh,

the Milwaukee sheik, took his 'cellar made' 45 Harley-Davidson over the wall in the 45 event. Which, of course, was considerable show for Art and his 'laboratory model.' "

This is an extremely interesting statement. Was Hap hinting that Earlenbaugh's "cellar made" bike was a 45 OHV that was not Home-Brew? Might not "laboratory model" be code for Harley's own experimental race shop? Was it coincidence that both Harley's experimental and racing departments during these years were indeed located downstairs in a "cellar" at Juneau Avenue?

Whatever their true background, by mid-1928 at least two nearly identical 45-cubic-inch Two-Cam/OHVs were being ridden by Milwaukee men with good factory connections. Apparently Harley-Davidson decided to keep these machines low key, opting not to officially publicize their experimental, quasi-factory status. That wouldn't be unusual for the secretive, sometimes unpredictable Motor Company.

In 1929, the Two-Cam/OHV temporarily fell by the wayside when the hot factory DAH began cleaning up the competition. But Bill Knuth wasn't done with the Two-Cam/OHV yet. After 1930 he used it as a basis for another 45 OHV hillclimber: "Knuth's Special."

What Knuth did (again probably with factory help) was saw off the cam chest on the Two-Cam bottom end and then weld on a four-camshaft cam chest removed from the D model 45-cubic-inch road bike. Ignition was by a rear-mounted magneto, chain driven from a sprocket mounted on the rear exhaust camshaft. The 21 OHV-style Peashooter heads were retained and may have been specially cast.

This four-camshaft layout gave Knuth's Special a straight pushrod angle, overhead-valves, and a racing-strength bottom end for a high-performance 45-cubic-inch motor. These were run in the proven FHAD hillclimb chassis. Chuck Wesholski, who has studied these motors, commented that "the Knuth Specials were *real* special, reflecting insider factory connections and a very intelligent and imaginative mechanical mind."

On a hillclimber all you had was a throttle and kill-button. The 1920s and early 1930s were the heyday of the slant artist.

While the transmission looks stock, hillclimb bikes were single-speed. Lever beneath the exhaust pipe is for putting the bike into gear. Hillclimb engine survival is high because bikes were built tough and runs lasted only 45 seconds or less.

Knuth's Specials were as good as factory hillclimbers. Accounts such as "Knuth's Klimbers are . . . copping all the bacon . . . riding Special 45 Harley-Davidson overhead jobs" were common fare in the motorcycle press. They allowed Bill Knuth to brag, "The[se] motors . . . are the most highly developed internal combustion engines in the world, developing about 1 horsepower per cubic inch and turning over as fast as 125 times per second."

No side-valve or F-head could match that. This gave Milwaukee plenty to chew on, because Harley-Davidson had more tricks up its sleeve.

CHAPTER 9
CHANGING TECHNOLOGY

The year 1929 was pivotal for Harley-Davidson. Three engine types were built: F-heads, side-valves, and overheads. But this was the last gasp for the F-head, and by 1931 the 21 OHV was gone too. By then, Harley's lineup was entirely devoted to the side-valve engine.

The side-valve seemed destined to rule forever. The Great Depression and a further decline in Motor Company profits seemed to ensure it. Behind the scenes, however, a different scenario was being played out at the Milwaukee factory.

In early 1929, H-D's engineering department graphed the horsepower curves of 15 models—from the 21 Single to the prototype VL. When Harley fans discuss this data, it's inevitably a shouting match over the performance merits of the JDH versus the VL. But that's like arguing about which dinosaur was baddest. The evolutionary winner was the little 21 OHV.

Although putting out just 12 peak horsepower, the 21 OHV did it with 350 cc, while it took the Big Twins a full 1,000 to 1,200 cc to make their 15 horsepower (Model J), 28 horsepower (prototype Model VL), or 29 horsepower (Model JDH). But *where* the 21 OHV made its power tells the full

story. While the D-, J-, and V-series bikes reached peak horsepower between 2,800 and 4,000 rpm, the little 21 OHV peaked at 4,800 rpm. After that its power fell off gradually compared to the F-head and side-valve motors, whose breathing ability fell off abruptly.

In fact, at 4,800 rpm, the J model's horsepower had fallen *below* that of the little 21 OHV. Even the horsepower of the new 45-cubic-inch side-valve came perilously close to 21 OHV levels at 4,800 rpm. The new C model—a 500 cc side-valve single—was 2 horsepower shy of 21 OHV peak output.

The superior breathing and winding characteristics of the overhead-valve engine weren't lost on Harley's engineers. They knew that if the Two-Cam/OHV or DAH hillclimb motors were plotted with those others, they'd blow the top off of the chart.

Always conservative Harley-Davidson, who for years painted their bikes duck boat green, now took a fresh look at the motorcycle market. If the VL was better than the Two-Cam JDH, it wasn't much better. The VL weighed more (528 pounds vs. 413 pounds by H-D's own specs) and still ran the archaic total-loss oiling system with its mysterious auxiliary handpump.

In spite of Harry Ricardo's work, the side-valve combustion chamber still had major defects. With its angles and corners and twists and turns

> ## "There is no argument but what we should have a faster . . . job."
>
> —Joe Ryan,
> H-D Service Manager

By the early 1930s, the side-valve engine carried the entire Harley-Davidson line. This 1933 VLD, owned by Mark Jonas, sports one of the more interesting paint jobs in H-D history.

you couldn't up the compression and still get it to breathe. Plus, the red hot exhaust valve sat next to the cylinder, causing it to locally overheat, warp, and eat pistons.

This letter to "Uncle Frank" (Hap Jameson) in *The Motorcyclist* is typical: "Uncle, my 1934-74 Harley has turned out to be a smelting furnace. She blew up the other day and upon taking off the cylinder heads I find that the front piston . . . looks like somebody got in there with a welding torch."

This wasn't the performance that riders expected from a motor Harley-Davidson advertised as having a "fighting heart." Riders wanted speed *and* reliability. Roads were rapidly improving, and the trend was toward fast solo bikes. Riders back then liked to "spank the saddle," especially after seeing an overhead-valve hillclimber go over the top.

Harley-Davidson was run by intelligent men. True motorcyclists. They saw the attention OHV race bikes received, and experience had shown the performance and reliability advantages of overhead valves. What better marriage between engineering and sales than to build a glamorous new overhead-valve twin?

Perhaps the original team of William S. Harley and Arthur Davidson—the head of engineering and the head of sales—came to the fore. As the Great Depression tightened its noose around Harley-Davidson, the founders shook the dice one last time when they decided to build a *real* sporting motorcycle, something modern and forward looking—and that meant overhead valves.

The groundwork had been laid with the Eight-Valve racers, the 21 OHV, and the 45 OHV hillclimbers. In 1929–1930, H-D built an experimental 30.50-cubic-inch (500 cc) OHV single with a recirculating oil system in road-bike trim. In 1930, they took the 45 OHV DAH hillclimb twin engine and modified it with a recirculating oil system. Then they stuffed it into a road-racing package as the DAR export model. With this bike, Harley-Davidson essentially created the Sportster 27 years ahead of schedule.

It's curious that Bill Harley's engineers didn't use the DAH/DAR engine as the basis for a road-legal overhead-valve twin. Maybe after experience with the 45 and 74 side-valves, they didn't like all those noisy, wear-prone

The VL engine was not totally satisfactory for high-speed work. Piston failure in the big side-valve engine was common, but few riders in the early 1930s imagined that the side-valve's days were numbered.

While a substantial and good-looking machine, the 45 side-valve wasn't much faster than the 21 OHV. This nice 36RLD1072 belongs to Mark Jonas.

angles. There is also great similarity between the shape of the JDH cam gear cover and that found on the Knucklehead, only slightly restyled and flipped around to the front. Even the Knucklehead's "diamond" primary chain cover is a modification of the earlier JD style.

Knowing how Harley did things, the many similar features between the Two-Cam/OHV and the Knucklehead are probably not coincidental. Most likely, Bill Harley and his engineers knew they could do better than the 4-camshaft layout used on the D, VL, and DAH, then cast around for a way out. The Two-Cam/OHV was fresh in mind and looked like a good place to start. Milwaukee was fond of the old F-head motor, especially in Two-Cam form. Its origin went back to 1903,

cam gears. Because when they began work on a "sump oiler" twin in 1931, they started with a blank sheet of paper—or did they?

Maybe not. If the thinking of some modern enthusiasts is correct, the inspiration for the Knucklehead engine may have come from a bike in Milwaukee's then recent past: the 1928 Two-Cam/OHV experimental hillclimber.

As no factory records have yet surfaced, this conclusion is still tentative. Those who worked on these bikes are all dead. But compare the Two-Cam/OHV with the 1936 EL model, and then decide for yourself. Placed side by side these two motors show hauntingly similar features.

Both machines have hemi-head, overhead-valve V-twin engines. Both share the paired detachable lifter blocks inherited from the JDH. Both display the same unique splayed pushrod

This later UL side-valve cut-a-way shows its simple but inefficient valve layout in an air-cooled engine. Exhaust valve location near the piston bore resulted in hot spots and premature piston failure. Motor courtesy Mike Lange.

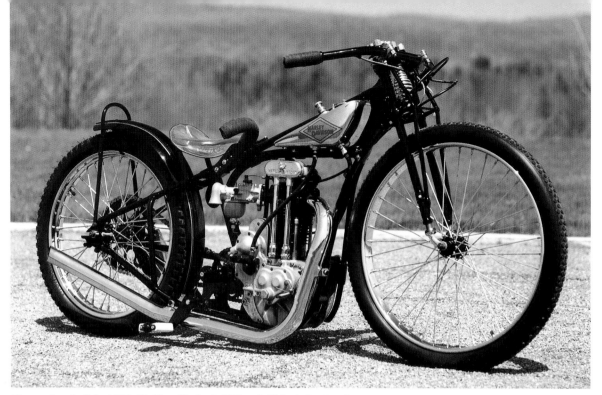

The engine in this 1934 30.50-cubic-inch (500 cc) CAC cinder-track racer was another step in H-D overhead-valve technology. David and Regina Hinze own this hot little racer.

The 1934 CAC has a more Knucklehead-like rocker housing instead of the plates formerly used on the 21 OHV and other Harley overheads. Owner R. L. Jones.

That was *their* motor. What better place to start when working up the Knucklehead?

Traditionally the VL has stood like a brick wall between the JDH Two-Cam and the 1936 EL model in the Big Twin's pedigree. With the Two-Cam/OHV hillclimber in the picture, however, we may have found the logical missing link in the Harley-Davidson line of descent, and thus the lost daddy of everyone's favorite old Harley: the Knucklehead.

Milwaukee may have built a machine even closer to the Knucklehead with the 1929 export FAR model. The FAR is a *real* mystery machine. It only appears on the 1929 list of factory racing bikes. In 1930, it was replaced with the four-camshaft DAR export road racer.

Being an F-series racing bike, the FAR would have used the Two-Cam bottom end. But it also had overhead-valves, as evidenced by the terse factory description: "29FAR 1000cc (61 cu. in.) 3 Speed Racer—Export (Overhead Valves)."

Here perhaps we find the ultimate Knucklehead ancestor. The FAR was 61 cubic inches—same

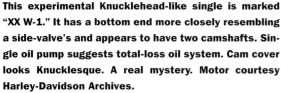

This experimental Knucklehead-like single is marked "XX W-1." It has a bottom end more closely resembling a side-valve's and appears to have two camshafts. Single oil pump suggests total-loss oil system. Cam cover looks Knucklesque. A real mystery. Motor courtesy Harley-Davidson Archives.

Larger head-finning on the Knuck single suggests stationary engine use. Most other parts differ from production ELs, often significantly. It's unclear how this factory experimental fits into the development of the EL, but it shows the direction Harley was moving by the early 1930s.

as the EL—and was set up as a road racer with a three-speed transmission. Possibly it ran a recirculating oil system. A sump oiler would make sense on a road racer. The DAR that replaced it had one.

Unfortunately, no further information or photo of the FAR is known to exist. We can only speculate

whether it was a sump oiler and whether its overhead-valve heads, cylinders, and pistons were lifted from the 1929 CA, a 30.50-cubic-inch (500 cc) OHV racing model. With a 4-inch stroke, this configuration would have yielded 60.12 cubic inches (985 cc) in a twin. It isn't difficult to imagine the

In 1936, H-D created a masterpiece with the 61 OHV, here illustrated by Mark Wall's superbly restored 36EL1002. Wall discovered this super-historic motorcycle in Wisconsin and brought it back to its original pristine condition.

boys at H-D trying the FAR prototype around Milwaukee and liking its gutsy potential very much.

If this theory is correct, Harley's talented engineers had little trouble redesigning these Two-Cam/OHV hybrids into a new motor. The prototype EL also included ideas from Bill Harley's own fertile mind. Noteworthy, was an elegant new camshaft arrangement and recirculating oil system, a patent for which was granted in 1938.

This artistic still life of a 1937 EL head, shows the 1936–1937-style "cup" enclosures around the valve springs. Cups and return oil lines to the rear side of rocker housing was a last-minute fix on the 1936 model. Note period tools.

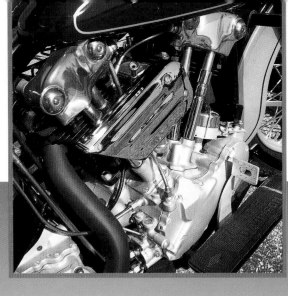

Early 1936 parts are clearly visible on 36EL1002. Until the mid-1950s, engine serial numbers began with "1000," thus this motor was the third EL assembled. Only discovery of the original 1903 prototype would surpass this machine's historical value.

Harley designers had gotten plenty of practice over the years, and the perfectly proportioned EL model shows it. Not registered in 1936, 36EL1002 appeared in 1937 with license plate number 52. In 1936, it may have been dealer Erik Eichmann's demonstrator in Sheboygan, Wisconsin.

In 1936, the big 80-cubic-inch VLH side-valve appeared. While a bigger engine, H-D test riders couldn't break 100 miles per hour with it. Scott Ranson owns this handsome example.

The new design was based on a four-lobed, single camshaft. This was a significant adaptation and improvement over the Two-Cam engine. The relocated and larger breather gear in the prototype EL supplied the cam lobes and roller tappets with many times the oil previously thought possible. The overhead-valve rocker arms were also oiled automatically. Just the ticket for a high-revving, high-performance overhead-valve engine. In this manner, Harley's pre-VL line of Big Twins metamorphosed into the immortal Knucklehead.

By using the Two-Cam/OHV as the basis for the 61 OHV, Bill Harley maintained the lineage of his original 1903 motor. Unlike previously thought, there was no break with the past. While new, the Knucklehead wasn't really new at all. And through the same evolutionary process, this continuity has remained true through subsequent motors to the present day.

CHAPTER 10

DREAM BABIES

The 61 OHV model introduced in 1936 was a combination of long experience and modern engineering. Testing Knucklehead prototypes EX-6 and 35EL1002 west of Jefferson, Wisconsin, in the summer of 1935, H-D test riders broke 100 miles per hour. The new 80-cubic-inch VLH side-valve wasn't capable of such speeds.

Later, Harley-Davidson revealed its overhead-valve strategy. "For years our engineers had a vision of a new motorcycle—one that would eliminate . . . the problems inherent with the conventional design of the day . . . that would retain all the best of the past and incorporate all those new principles that would produce a motorcycle unparalleled in performance and efficiency."

In the 61 OHV, riders found their dream come true. The first unveiling came at the Harley-Davidson dealers' convention at Milwaukee in late 1935. Advance billing for this national conference, the first in five years, made the dealers nuts for something new—and they got it.

The late Tom Vandegrift, then dealer in Albert Lea, Minnesota, recalled in a 1997 interview: "It was announced we would have a sensation. They had everybody's vision setting on there. Then they pulled the cover off it. We always expected to see something new, but that 61 was radically different

This exquisite 36EL, owned by George and Kathy Pardos, sports the deluxe chrome package. In the minds of many Harley enthusiasts, the styling peak attained in 1936 has never been surpassed.

because it was an overhead. Afterwards everybody got in there and crowded around so that you couldn't get at it."

Almost every part on the 61 OHV was new. The only things recognizable from the VL were the fenders and generator. The new double-cradle frame divorced the EL from the old loop-frame days forever. The fork went back to the 21 Single's tubular style, beefed up for Big Twin duty. Tires were 4.00x18s, as found on the 45 twin.

The new transmission was the traditional Harley gearbox revamped into an indestructible, constant-mesh four-speed. Built-in instruments formed Bill Harley's patented integral dash. The combined oil tank/battery box was another patented feature. The gas tanks were sleek, teardrop-shaped units—so impressive that H-D still uses them today. The engine can only be described as a masterpiece of performance, reliability, and mechanical beauty.

"This is a 5,000 rpm motor."
—Uncle Frank

While the younger dealers marveled at this glittering new apparition of the motorcycle world, the older dealers nodded and smiled, knowing that in the 61 OHV, the king of motorcycles had been reborn.

Reborn because old-timers recalled the famous overheads of their youth—dealers such as Dudley Perkins, who handled the futuristic Jefferson OHV before he became a Harley dealer. Uncrating a new Jefferson twin in 1913, he found it good for 78 miles per hour—not bad when the hot 1928–1929 JDH Two-Cam topped out at 85.

At the evening banquet, tales of early American overheads filled the room—ghostly names such as Breed, Royal Pioneer, Jefferson, Kenzler-Waverley, P.E.M., Pope, and the fantastic overhead-valve, overhead-camshaft Cyclone. Behind these nostalgic musings was the joy that in the 61 OHV this superior engine type had come round again.

No test rides were allowed at the November conference, probably because the engineering and

Carburetor-cover style was unique to 1936. Compare the cam-gear cover here and on 36EL1002 to see progression within the 1936 model year. Small chain and round device below kick pedal are brake light parts.

experimental departments were still frantically developing an oil recovery system for the exposed valve stems and springs. Yet, on the basis of a single look, many dealers placed orders for the new EL.

Another superb Mark Wall restoration is 36EL2517. In the optional Maroon-with-Nile green paint scheme, this bike is incredibly flashy and good looking even with very little chrome, and would be the centerpiece of any antique Harley collection.

The styling of the 36EL wasn't slack from any angle. No motorcycle in history had such a long, thoughtful development and subsequent influence. This model links the original Harley-Davidson Motor Co. with today's bikes.

One was Bill Borer, the LaCrosse, Wisconsin, dealer who, mere hours after the November event, was hollering at Art Blixt for an EL. On December 6, Blixt wrote back, "I haven't seen a single 61 shipment as yet on any of the factory daily shipping lists which I receive every day." Borer had to wait for this later note from Joe Kilbert, "We shipped you a 61 overhead on January 17."

This narrows the long-held controversy as to when the first ELs left the Milwaukee factory. Records from Guy Webb's St. Paul dealership show that 36EL1137 and 36EL1144 were shipped on January 24. These dates jibe with the first public notice of a 61 in the *Enthusiast*, telling of a February 2 win at an Oregon endurance run.

As Harley serial numbers started with 1000, this leaves the first 138 61 OHV motors (those below 36EL1137) to account for. It's doubtful that large a number was shipped before January 17. These were probably held back for refitting with the last-minute fix of oil cups and return lines. This cured the original messy arrangement of oil applied directly to bare valve parts exposed to the airstream. Some old-timers recall early 36EL heads being replaced by the factory. Mystery surrounds the first Knucklehead.

Harley-Davidson furthered the EL's mystique by first playing the 61 OHV cautiously and then bragging about it afterwards. In February, the factory warned dealers only to sell the new model to those who would have nothing else. Joe Kilbert counseled them in a letter. "If you have any prospects who will . . . quit [riding] . . . unless they can get a job like the 61, by all means, sell them the 61 o.h.v."

By April, delivery time of 61s had improved to two weeks, although dealers were warned *"not to go out and sell a lot of 61s."* By July, an unexpected demand for the established models made delivery time for the 61 OHV even better. William H.

continued on page 88

In 1937, the big side-valves were updated with the EL recirculating oil system, and 61 styling. This well-accessorized 1937 UH belongs to Dale Cashman.

Mark Jonas' 37EL1970 shows the oil tank painted to match the bike's gas tanks, which was unique to that year. A nice touch but tough to keep clean. Authentic restorations rely on rich paint and the sheer mechanical beauty of the original design.

Joe Petrali's record breaker, inside H-D Archives. This bike did 136.183 miles per hour at Daytona in 1937. It runs a 1915 fork, JD wheels, and hand-built frame. H-D's Ray Schlee, when cleaning the bike, saved the Daytona Beach sand caught in the frame. The original seat and fender are missing.

The 1939 Knuckleheads had a nice two-tone paint job that Harley has been using again recently. This was the last year of the lean 1930s look for the 61 OHV. The bike is 39EL2305, owned by Mark Jonas.

The only rival to the 61 OHV in Harley's line-up was the 80-cubic-inch ULH side-valve Sport Solo. While massive, the 80 couldn't match the smaller 61 in sustained high-speed durability. Owner of 40ULH4606 is Mark Jonas.

The big side-valve engine was easy starting, distinctive looking, and good for low- to mid-speed work. But by 1941, the overhead twins were outselling the big side-valves.

By 1941, H-D engineering reached another plateau. The 45 engine would change little over the next three decades until its retirement in the 1970s. Mark Jonas owns 41WLD7327.

You have to look twice to see the difference between the 45 and Big Twin side-valves. The two bikes looked similar except that the rear chains came off opposite sides.

continued from page 83

Davidson, who was then in sales, wrote, "Dealers can get 61s . . . on very short notice. . . . (that) gives us a chance to utilize the . . . side valve models . . . for police and commercial sales."

In spite of a few inevitable first year flaws, the 61 OHV performed well. Its quick acceptance by dealers and riders alike, delighted the factory. Confidence rising, Milwaukee crowed with typical 1930s Harley-Davidson bombast: "With years of development behind the new model . . . with 70,000 hours of testing, we knew we were bringing out a new motorcycle that would eclipse everything ever produced before."

What the factory didn't mention, however, was that Lothar A. Doerner, William S. Harley's "right-hand assistant" during the EL's creation, was killed that July testing a new 1937 model near Wisconsin's little Mississippi River town of Victory.

Unlike the 21 OHV, whose quiet introduction in 1926 was followed by a phasing out a few years later, the 61 OHV took hold and never let go. In 1937, the side-valves were redesigned along 61 OHV lines. But while the UL (74 cubic inches) and ULH (80 cubic inches) were nice bikes if not pushed hard, extinction for the big side-valve was on the horizon. As early as February 1936, *Bill Knuth's Tattler* said, "George Feith is getting an 80 in maroon and cream and looking forward to a race with Kelly to decide whether the 61 really has it over the 80. Who will win?"

Harley-Davidson already knew the answer. One factory guy wrote to dealers in 1936, "Here is a model that the motorcycle enthusiast takes right to his heart. It has the class, the lines, the features that make a motorcycle enthusiast want to say— 'How much will you allow me on my hack for one of these dream babies?'"

At the Milwaukee factory this change was soon evident. In 1936, the only Harley *or* Davidson with a 61 OHV registered for street use was William J. Harley (Bill Harley's older son), who

This style dash went back to 1939. The classic Harley layout that originated with the 36EL is evident on Jonas' 41WLD. Tank-mounted speedo and ignition switch grace Harley models today, as well as new copycat bikes.

Only a few 1942 civilian models were built. This 74 OHV, photographed at Davenport, is one of about 800 FLs built that year. Big tires and metal tank badges took away from earlier sleek looks of 1930s EL models.

had 36EL1517. By late 1940, however, Walter C. Davidson was riding 40EL1420; William J. Harley, 40EL3157; William H. Davidson, 40E3185; and John Harley, 41FL3900. Only Gordon Davidson stuck to the flathead—40U2496.

Numbers tell the tale. In 1936, H-D built "nearly 2,000" 61 OHVs. (Factory sources state 1,704 while serial number analysis suggests nearer 1,950.) That same year 5,480 big side-valves left the factory. By 1941, 5,149 EL and FL overheads were built compared to 4,145 big side-valves. That year just 420 80-cubic-inch Special

Sport Solo ULH models were built—the OHV twins' only real competition.

With the coming of the 74 OHV in 1941, the big flathead was doomed. Ironically, it also killed the 61 OHV. Connie Schlemmer, who worked at Otto Ramer's Omaha dealership in the 1930s, recalled. "We had one fellow [Fave] who would order a new 61 every year. . . . In 1940 he . . . was talking with Hap Jameson [who] offered to take [Fave's] buddy seat passenger in his sidecar, which was hooked to a prototype 74 OHV engine, and Fave said he could hardly keep up with the sidecar with his 61."

89

Still riding. Bruce Linsday with his 1937 Knucklehead. He took a 38EL to Germany, then rode it to Russia and back. These bikes run!

After the FL was introduced in 1941, sales of the EL dropped off drastically. In 1952 (their last year), only 960 61 OHV Panheads were built compared to 5,740 74 OHVs.

Some thought the EL was smoother and went fast enough. One modern rider who agrees is Bruce Linsday. Probably the most dedicated Knucklehead fan alive, Linsday rides his original

Close-up of a 74-cubic-inch OHV engine shows the mighty Knucklehead at its peak. No other design has shown such staying power; indeed, Harley motors today are still based on the Knucklehead.

1937 and 1938 ELs like most guys *don't* ride their new bikes. He's crossed the country at least 15 times on Knuckleheads. If that wasn't enough, he and his girlfriend once took his 1938 EL to Germany and rode to Moscow and back.

"I think it's the best thing Harley *ever* did," Linsday said. "The 61 was a better combination than the 74. The 61 had the small diameter flywheels and the 18-inch [road] wheels. The bigger [16-inch] tire made them handle like a tank. It was no improvement. Those 61 Knuckleheads are smooth and well balanced. They're an amazingly good engine. . . . I'm still impressed by them."

THE GHOST IN THE MACHINE

In the 36EL and 41FL models lays the combined genius of those thousands of Harley-Davidson workers who reached the peak of their talents in the 1920s and 1930s. With the Knucklehead, the founders immortalized in iron their concept of the ideal motorcycle.

Yet the 61 and 74 OHV models could trace their origin directly back to the 1903 prototype, which over the decades had been updated and improved, and in 1928 was converted to full overhead-valve in the experimental Two-Cam/OHV hillclimber. This bike in turn inspired the 1936 and 1941 Knuckleheads—the first real overhaul of the Harley-Davidson motorcycle since 1903.

This 1915 twin shows original inlet-over-exhaust valve (F-head) layout used on all pre-1930 Big Twins. With a few changes you'd have the original 1903 motor. Engine courtesy Mike Lange.

> ## "It is hard to tell if we adore these old bikes because they have a soul or because they assist us with ours."
>
> ### —Martin Jack Rosenblum

The Knucklehead came none too soon: by 1950, the four founders of Harley-Davidson were dead. By then much had changed. Another world war had come and gone. The competition had a new face. Riders and bikes were changing too. America was entering the modern era.

Yet the founders' final and greatest creation lived on. For the Knucklehead embodied more than just good looks and sustainable high speed. It was the first Harley-Davidson with timeless appeal. Call it what you want—heritage, prestige, mystique, nostalgia, work-of-art, soul, spirit, daemon, orenda, kami, or dream baby—it's all the same. It's the truth behind the slogan "More than a machine," or more poetically perhaps: *the ghost in the machine.*

It's what drives some to adorn their bodies with Harley-Davidson symbols. Why Japanese enthusiasts—countrymen of the builders of the

The Two-Cam was the next step in Big Twin evolution. This 1924 example is the "indirect-action" type with cam followers and cast-in tappet guides. Engine courtesy R. L. Jones.

Electra-Glide. Plus the choppers, the factory customs, the Springers, the Fat Boys, and the Bad Boys. Then toss in the dizzying array of Japanese, American, and European copycat bikes. No matter what name, insignia, or slogan they hide behind, the Knucklehead inspired them all.

The current Motor Company knows it. They know they must retain the mystique of Bill Harley's 1936 creation while competing against

world's most advanced double overhead-camshaft, many-cylinder, multi-valve, liquid cooled, computerized, fuel-injected, shaft-drive motorcycles—unexpectedly reject their own techno wonders for an admittedly antiquated Harley-Davidson, essentially the same machine that Bill Harley breathed life into in 1936. Why? As one Japanese rider put it, "My Harley-Davidson is alive."

The Knucklehead is the greatest motorcycle of them all. One has only to look at the present generation of Harley-Davidson Big Twins to see that. The 36EL sired the Panhead, the Shovelhead, the Evolution, and the new Twin Cam 88 motor. It begat the Hydra-Glide, the Duo-Glide, and the

Experimental 45-cubic-inch Two-Cam/OHV hillclimber engine mated Peashooter heads to the Two-Cam bottom end. Cylinders were specially cast. This 1928 Two-Cam bottom is the "direct-action" type with detachable tappet blocks and no cam followers. Bike courtesy Motorcycle Heritage Museum.

This 1936 EL engine (in George and Kathy Pardos' machine) shows hauntingly similar features to the Two-Cam/OHV, although refined and modernized. Decide for yourself whether the Two-Cam/OHV is the missing link in the Big Twin line.

the increasingly sophisticated competition in the 21st century. They realize the stakes. As H-D's head engineer, Earl Werner, said recently, "Trying to innovate while preserving the purity in the heritage. It weighs heavily on all of us."

Harley-Davidson grabbed both future and past with its new 1999 model Twin Cam 88 engine. At first glance the new dual-camshaft layout seems a taboo break with tradition, but clearly, when one studies Harley's past, it is not. We only have to go back to the progenitor of the Knucklehead—the 1928 experimental Two-Cam/OHV hillclimber—to find what Harley engineers reinvented today.

Coincidence? Maybe. Or maybe the ghost is real after all. Maybe Bill Harley and the Davidson brothers still haunt the bricks and mortar of Juneau Avenue. Maybe, in whispered dreams, they're still calling the shots.

BIBLIOGRAPHY

Bach, Sharon and Ken Ostermann. *The Legend Begins, Harley-Davidson Motorcycles, 1903–1969*. Milwaukee: Harley-Davidson, Inc., 1993.

Bolfert, Thomas C. *The Big Book of Harley-Davidson*. Milwaukee: Harley-Davidson, Inc., 1989.

The Enthusiast. Milwaukee: Harley-Davidson Motor Co.

Field, Greg. *Harley-Davidson Knuckleheads*. Osceola: MBI Publishing Company, 1997.

Hatfield, Jerry. *American Racing Motorcycles*. Osceola: MBI Publishing Company, 1989.

Hatfield, Jerry. *Inside Harley-Davidson*. Osceola: MBI Publishing Company, 1990.

Hatfield, Jerry. *Illustrated Antique American Motorcycle Buyer's Guide*. Osceola: MBI Publishing Company, 1996.

Hendry, Maurice D. *Harley-Davidson*. New York: Ballantine Books, 1972.

The Milwaukee Journal. Milwaukee.

MotorCycling. Chicago.

The Motorcyclist. Los Angeles.

Wagner, Herbert. *Harley-Davidson 1930–1941*. Atglen: Schiffer Ltd., 1996.

INDEX